A DICTIONARY OF CORK SLANG

SEÁN BEECHER was a friend and a good writer. He was a folklorist, a
lover of the Irish language, a great GAA man and a local historian of
some note. He was a quiet-spoken man with a terrific Cork lilt. He was
proud of everything he did, his connections, his Cork roots.

The historical treasure trove in Cork fascinated him. He had a
keen interest in the city's roots, its development and its distinctive language.

His interests did not make Seán a wealthy man – he was never in
it for the money. He did what he did because of his love for the subject
matter. By the time of his death Seán had also written *The Story of Cork,
Day by Day – a Miscellany of Cork History, The Blues: A History of St
Finbarr's in Cork, The Fastnet File* and *An Gaeilge in Cork City*. He will be
missed.

DICK HOGAN, *The Irish Times*, January 1998

To Heather,
This might help you to
understand / translate me a bit
more!/ :-)
DAVE

A DICTONARY
of
CORK SLANG

Seán Beecher

The Collins Press

This edition in 1991 by
The Collins Press
West Link Park
Doughcloyne
Wilton
Cork

Reprinted 1996, 1999, 2004

First published by Goldy Angel Press 1983

British Library Cataloguing in Publication data.

Cover design: Artmark

Printed in Ireland by Colour Books Ltd.

ISBN: 0-951603-61-2

ACKNOWLEDGEMENTS

I would like to express my thanks to the many individuals who helped in the preparation of this book. I was delighted to find that people, whom I hardly knew gave generously of their time and expertise. If their advice was not always taken, if I chose to deviate from their exacting academic standards, it was because it afforded me a freedom to speculate freely on meanings and interpretations.

An t-Ollamh Pádraigh Ó Riain and Gearóid Ó Crualaoich of University College, Cork, read the manuscript and made many very valuable suggestions. I am indebted to Pól Ruiséal of An Teanglann, U.C.C., who prepared the phonetic form of the words. It was not possible, for technical reasons, to include them in the script and Peter Varian was generous enough to transcribe them on to the manuscript. Max McCarthy of the College library also provided me with books.

I could not have completed the book without the help and co-operation of Tim Cadogan of the Cork County Library. He provided me with books, suggested many sources, and was always patient and courteous. My old friend, Caoimhín Ó Súilleabháin, read the drafts, researched sources, and was always encouraging, as was John O'Mahony who listened patiently to my explanations. Jimmy-Barry Murphy also read the drafts and suggested many words, as did my mother and Noreen, Arthur Moynihan, Tim Daly, Donie Cremin and Mick Collins.

My brother, Jim in London, checked the manuscript against Wright's English Dialect Dictionary, that particular tome not being available in Cork. Esther Diggin somehow deciphered my handwriting and typed the manuscript. And finally, I would like to thank my wife, Sheila, who tolerated many inconveniences and procrastinations and always encouraged me to complete the book.

SEÁN BEECHER

AISH, noun

A character, a person.

Use: He's a tough aish =
He's a tough individual.

Derivation: See 'Aos' – people, folk, generation. Dinneen. 'Aes' – age, folk. Kuno Meyer. 'Éis' (Bearlagar na Saer) – a man. MacAlister.

BAA, ALL A

Exclamation by player about to make off with stake-money in games of cards or feck (see). The phrase 'All-a-baa' is said at the precise moment the money is grabbed. It is usually preceded (thus giving warning of the attempt) by a further phrase 'Sheep on the mountain'. Accordingly, the full phrase would be 'Sheep on the mountain all-a-baa!' It was considered an unorthodox but not illegal way of recovering losses.

Derivation unknown.

BACK, OWN, noun

Revenge, retribution.

Use: I'll get me own back on him someday =
I'll get my revenge on him someday.

Derivation unknown.

BACK-BERIL, noun and verb

Opposite spinning motion to 'Beril' (which see). This technique was not usually permitted.

Derivation unknown.

BAKE, noun

A fiasco; a disappointment (film, theatre).
Use: The film was a bake =
The film was a disappointment.
Derivation doubtful.
Note: *Bacach* = defective, imperfect. Dineen.

BAND-HOUSE PLAYER, noun

Bad card-player.
Derivation: Old men played cards, usually 'Don' (which see) in the Old Band House in the Mardyke (opposite College entrance). The stake was one farthing a 'Corner' (see). The standard of play was bad – hence 'A band-house player'.

BAREAAS, noun

Bare feet.
Use: The children are in their bareaas all through the summer =
The children do not wear shoes during the summer.
Derivation: Corruption of 'bare' and addition of colloquial 'as'.

BANKS, DOWN THE, verb

Reprimand.
Use: I gave him down the banks =
I criticized him severely.
Derivation: Unknown, but note 'Reprimand – scolding, punishment of any kind'. Joyce.

BASKET, noun

A loaf of bread shaped like a basket.
Derivation unknown.

BATE, noun

A piece or slice (of bread).

Derivation: Possibly Old Norse 'Beita' (to cause to bite). Chambers.

BATTER, noun

A drinking spree.

Use: I was on a fierce batter last week =
I was on a prolonged drinking spree last week.

Derivation: Concise Oxford Dictionary – spree or binge (origin unknown).

See 'a riotous spree'. Partridge.

BATTLE-BOARD, noun

Salted fish – usually cod or ling.

Derivation possibly from Battle, meaning nourishing, from Old Norse 'Batt'. Chambers.

BAYTUR, noun

A foolish person.

Use: Go away, you baytur =
Go away, you fool.

Derivation: Doubtful, but see 'Báethare', zany, baethar, a fool. Kuno Meyer.

BAZER, noun

A blow.

Use: He gave him a bazer =
He struck him a blow

Derivation: Unknown, but note 'Baiser' (French) a kiss, a salute. Cassells.

and note 'Bazz' – to thrash or to beat. Wright.

BAZZ, noun
Pubic hair.
Derivation unknown.

BAZZER, noun
Haircut.
Use: I got a bazzer yesterday =
I got a haircut yesterday.
Derivation: Unknown, but see 'Bazz' above.

BELLISITUPUM, verb
To humiliate (sporting context) to inflict a heavy defeat on the opponents.
Use: Bellisitupum now ! =
Beat them decisively, score many goals, etc.
Derivation: Probably corruption of 'Bellows it up them'.

BEE-UP, noun
A game, similar to 'Feck' (which see). The players pitch (see) coins to a jack (which see), the closeness of the coins to the jack determines the order of tossing the coins. The person tossing bets on his own 'heads'. If the coins turn up 'heads', he wins whatever bets he made and tossed again and repeated until the coins turned up 'harps' (or tails). Each player takes his turn to bet against the man tossing in the same order as the proximity of his coin to the 'jack'.
Derivation unknown.

BERIL, noun and verb
The act of turning a coin on its own axis in anti-clockwise direction while tossing. Phrase used in context of game of 'Feck' and 'Bee-up' (which see). Opposite to 'Back-beril' (which see).
Derivation: Unknown, but note 'Birl' (Scots).

8

BING-BING, noun
Rapid turning of coin on its own axis when being 'tossed'. Effected by resting coin on index finger and spinning it by striking with thumb-nail. Usually regarded as being against the rules.
Derivation: Unknown, but possibly related to sound of coin spinning on the ground.

BLACKAS, noun
Blackberries.
Derivation: Local practice of abbreviating words.

BOCKETY, adjective
Crooked, out of alignment.
Use: One of the table legs is bockety =
One of the table legs is crooked – meaning short.
Derivation: Probably from Irish 'Bacac' – imperfect, defective. Dinneen.
Also note 'Bockady' – a lame person. Joyce.

BODICE, noun
Pig meat – spare ribs.
Derivation: Unknown, possibly from similarity of shape to whalebone stays in woman's bodice.

BOLGER, noun
Cranky individual.
Derivation unknown.

BOOK, noun

Class in school (Primary).
Hence third book = third class.
Out of books = finished school.
Derivation: Probably from the time when one textbook
contained material for study during one school year.

BOWLS, GAME OF, noun

A game played in Counties Cork and Armagh. It is played on
the roads, a twenty-eight ounce iron ball being thrown along
the road from one point to another (about three miles apart),
the player to cover the distance in the least number of throws
being declared the winner.

BOWL, ALONG, noun

A provocative remark (neither serious nor malicious).
Use: 'Now there's a long bowl' =
That is a provocative remark.
Derivation: See 'Bowls, Game of'.

BOWL OF ODDS, noun

A substantial advantage (term in game of bowls). When a
player's bowl is ahead of another, while he has yet a throw in
reserve.
Derivation: From term used in game of bowls (see).

BOX, ON THE, adverb

Copulating, having intercourse.
Use: I was on the box last night =
I had intercourse last night.
Derivation unknown.

BRAG, THREE-CARD, noun

A card game played by as many as seventeen players, each player receiving three cards – related to 'Niner' (which see).
Derivation: Unknown, but note 'A game at cards, so called because the players brag of their cards to induce the company to make bets'. Brewer.

BRASSED-OFF, adjective

Tired, bored.
Use: I'm brassed-off with nothing to do =
I'm fed-up because I have nothing to do.
Derivation: Unknown, but note 'Brass off' – to grumble (military). Partridge.
and impudence, audacity. Wright.

BRASSER, noun

A prostitute.
Use: That wan is a brasser =
That girl is a prostitute.
Derivation: Possibly from Irish 'Brasaire' – a flatterer. Dinneen.
French 'Embrasser' – to embrace, to clasp, to kiss. Cassells.

BROWL, noun

A stupid or foolish person, a blunderer.
Use: Don't be doing the browl =
Don't be acting the ignoramus.
Derivation: Possibly from Irish 'Breall' – a fool's mistake. Dinneen.
Also Irish 'Brell' – an object of disgrace, a mocking stock. Meyer.
And see – Irish 'Briulla Nó Brealla',
Duine nea-thuisgineach, duine gan puinn céile – a person without sense. Ó Briain.
'Browl' (Cumbria and Yorkshire, England) – An impudent rude child, saucy, impertinent. Wright.

11

BRUS, noun

Small pieces (of a broken object).

Use: The vase fell from the shelf and was in brus =
The vase fell from the shelf and was broken into
smithereens.

Derivation: Probably Irish 'Brus' – small fragments. Dinneen.
From 'Brúscar' – bits, crumbs, fragments. Meyer.

BRUS, noun

Fragments of boiled sweets, sold cheaply as 'Brus'.

Use: I have a lop for brus =
I have a penny to buy broken sweets.

Derivation: See 'Brus' above.

BURN, noun

A disappointment.

Use: He got a bad burn when his fiancée jilted him =
He got a bad disappointment when his fiancée jilted him.

Derivation unknown.

BUTT, noun

A cart.

Use: Tackle up the donkey and butt and we'll go to the fair =
Tackle up the donkey and cart and we'll go to the fair.

Derivation: 'A sort of cart, boarded at bottom and all around
the sides, fifteen to eighteen inches deep. In Cork, any kind of
horse-cart or donkey-cart is called a butt'. Joyce.

CAFFLER, noun

A young rogue, an impish, saucy young fellow, an impertinent boy.

Use: That fellow is a caffler =
That fellow is a rogue, he is saucy, impertinent.

Derivation: Probably French 'Caviller'.

And note 'Caffler – from Caviller' – a contemptible little fellow who gives saucy, cheeky, foolish talk. Joyce

See ' . . . . I rocked that little caffler in his cradle'. Murphy.

See 'Young cafflers would come after me along the Mardyke calling me names'. O'Mahony.

CALL, verb

To declare invalid the tossing of the coins during a game of feck. Each player being allowed one 'Call'. The coins are re-tossed. Betting is invalid on a 'Call'.

Use: Call 'em, i.e. toss them once more.

Derivation: Possibly from Irish 'Call' – defect, hence to rectify defect. Dineen.

CALL, noun and verb

The act of buying a round of drinks in a pub; buying thus.

Use: 'Your call' =
Your turn to get the round of drinks.

Derivation unknown.

CALL, A NOBLE, noun

The right of a singer at party to nominate the next performer.

Use: You have a noble call =
You are entitled to nominate the next singer.

Derivation unknown.

CALL, noun

Right (used in negative context).

Use: You had no call to do that =
You had no right to do that.

Derivation: Irish 'Call' – right.
'Níl aon call agat dó' – No right to it. Ó Domhnaill.
Irish 'Cál' – right, relationship.
'Níl aon cál'. Ó Briain.

Call, noun

A demand.

Use: There's a great call for that service =
There's a great demand for that service.

Derivation unknown.

CARRYING

To have money in one's possession.

Use: Are you carrying ? =
Do you have money in your possession ?

Derivation unknown.

CAT AND DOG, noun

A game.

Cat and dog was played on the streets with two sticks; the larger – the dog, was held in the hand, the smaller – the cat, was on the ground. It had tapered ends so it hopped into the air when struck at either end. Extensively played in India and probably brought to Cork by the Munster Fusiliers. Game called 'Tip-Cat' in England; 'Gillibanda' in India. Concise Oxford Dictionary.

Also played in various forms in other countries – 'Cattie and Doggie' in Scotland. Wright.

CAWHAKE, noun

Ill-luck.

Use: Someone put the cawhake on that job =
Someone put a jinx on that job.

Derivation: Possibly Irish 'Cáech' – blighted, marred, spoiled. Meyer.

CAWHAKE, noun

A peculiar individual.

Use: He's a cawhake, that fellow =
He's a peculiar individual.

Derivation: Doubtful, but see 'Cawhake' above.

CHANEYS, noun

Bits of pottery used in games played by young girls.

Derivation: Probably corruption of 'china', pottery.

Note 'Chanies' – used as money in children's games. Brady.

CHANEY-EYE, noun

False eye.

See 'Chaneys'.

Derivation: False eyes were made from porcelain, hence china and 'chaney-eye'.

CHAW, TO . . . . OUT, verb

To abuse verbally, to castigate.

Use: He chawed me out =
He castigated me.

Derivation: Possibly Old English to chew, to bite, hence to chaw out, to abuse. Concise Oxford Dictionary.

CHOICER, FOR, noun
Free gratis – for nothing.
Use: I got that for choicer =
I got that for nothing.
Derivation unknown.

CLAIM, verb
To challenge.
Use: I claimed him =
I challenged him to fight.
Derivation: See 'to seize, to arrest'. Partridge.

CLICK, verb
To succeed in attracting the attention of a member of the opposite sex.
Use: Did you click her? =
Did you pick her up?
A successful meeting with an unknown member of the opposite sex.
Derivation: Partridge.

CLING, verb
To fight.
Use: They were clung out of each other =
They were fighting.
Derivation: Unknown, but probably to describe a struggle between people.
Note 'To rush with violence'. *Morte d'Arthur.* Wright.

16

CLOD, noun
A penny.
Derivation unknown.

CLOUT, noun and verb
A heavy blow with the hand (or object), to strike.
Use: I gave him a clout of the hurley =
I struck him with the hurley.
Derivation: Irish 'Clabhta' – a blow with the open hand.
Dinneen.
and 'A heavy blow with some object in the hand' – now more
usual. Ó h-Éaluithe.
and 'Clout' – to hit, especially with open hand. Old English
'Clút'. Concise Oxford Dictionary.
and 'Clout' – to strike a person heavily. Middle English
onwards, now colloquial. Partridge.

COBBAGE, noun
A kind of commission on a transaction obtained by the 'go-
between' who deducted his payment from the amount of the
deal, usually without the explicit approval of the main parties,
but with their implicit consent.
Use: Did you make any cobbage ? =
Did you make money on the deal ?
Derivation unknown.

COCKER, noun
When a coin tossed during a game of feck lodged on its edge in
the ground and remains on edge, it is called a 'Cocker' *i.e.* it
does not indicate decisively either 'head' or 'harp' (or tails)
and the coin must be tossed again.
Derivation: Unknown, but note 'used to tilt of various
things, *e.g.* a hat'. Wright.

COD, noun and verb

To deceive, to joke, a fraud.

Use: You can't cod me =
You can't fool me.
or
I was only codding =
I was only joking.

Derivation: Irish 'Cadaráil' – foolish prattling. Dinneen.

English – nonsense, hoax, parody, from 'cods-wallop' (origin unknown). Concise Oxford Dictionary.

To chaff, hoax, play the fool. Partridge.

Note 'Codderauling' – idle gossip, prattle. Ó h-Éaluithe.

and see 'Who are you codding ?'. O'Mahony.

CODGER, noun

A foolish person.

Use: 'Isn't it awful ?', he would say, 'what a man has to put up with from an ould codger like him'. Murphy.

Derivation: See 'Cod' above.

and note Turkish 'Kodjah' – an old man or woman. Brewer.

COLLAR, verb

To capture, to take possession of, to seize, to appropriate.

Use: ' . . . . There's no shaking them off 'til they've collared a good portion' =
. . . . There's no shaking them off 'til they've appropriated a good portion. Murphy.

Derivation: English 'to seize' from Old French 'Colier' and Latin 'Collars'. Concise Oxford Dictionary.

and note 'To collar one is to seize by the collar, to appropriate without leave'. Brewer.

COLLOPS, noun

The calves of the legs.

Use: She has a fine pair of collops on her =
   She has large rounded calves.

Derivation: Irish 'Colpach' – having stout calves or legs. Dinneen.

Irish 'Colptha' – the calf of the leg. Meyer.

Collop – a slice of meat (Scandinavian origin). Concise Oxford Dictionary.

CONJUN-BOX, noun

A savings box used by children usually made in the shape and colour of post-box or pillar-box.

Derivation: Possibly from Tamil 'Kanji' – a lock-up (military), hence a place to keep money; possibly introduced into Cork by the Munster Fusiliers.

CONNIHALY, noun

Penis (usually in reference to a boy or young child).

Use: His poor old connihaly is sore =
   His penis is sore.

Derivation: Unknown, but may refer to an individual named Connie Healy who had a small penis.

CONNISHUR, noun and verb

A gossip, to gossip (maliciously).

Use: She's an awful connishur =
She's a persistent gossip.

Derivation: Uncertain, probably a local corruption of connoisseur.

COP-ON (TO), noun and verb
To understand, understanding.
Use: He has great cop-on =
He has great understanding.
also 'cop-on' as in
He has copped-on to it =
He has grasped its significance.
Derivation unknown.

COTTAGE, noun
A loaf of bread of a distinctive shape.
Derivation unknown.

COUGH, TO SOFTEN, verb
To chastise, to bring a person down a peg, to deflate.
Use: That will soften his cough =
That will deflate him.
Derivation unknown.

COWLUCK, noun
Derelict site in the city, generally due to the demolition of buildings.
Use: We were playing in the cowluck =
We were playing in the derelict site.
Derivation: Probably Irish 'Cabhlach' – the walls and frame of a house. Dinneen.

CRABBIT, adjective
Cunning, smart (derogatory).
Use: He's crabbit =
He's cute, smart.
Derivation unknown.

CRACKAWLY, adjective

Stupid.

Use: He's crackawly =
He is a stupid person.

Derivation: Possibly Old English 'Crack' – a crazy or soft-headed person. The Irish 'Ealaí' may have been added. Partridge.

Note 'Crackaulee' – a giddy young person of destructive habits, or 'Creacaill' – a person of cross disposition; also 'Creachaille' perhaps 'Creach aillidhe' (unwarranted suffix of agency) or English 'Crack-all'.

Note 'Craiceálaí' (Waterford). Ó h-Éaluithe.

CRAW-SICK, noun

Sick, nauseous (after a night's drinking).

Use: I was feeling craw-sick this morning =
I was feeling very sick (from drink) this morning.

Derivation: Possibly from craw – the human neck or throat, hence craw-sick.

"Crawsick

DAWFAKE, verb
To counterfeit, to alter.
Use: He dawfaked the driving licences =
He altered the driving licences.
Derivation unknown.

DALK, noun and verb
A blow, to strike.
Use: I gave him a dalk =
I struck him with my fist.
Derivation: Possibly Irish 'Dealg' – a thorn, hence a prick, a
blow. Dinneen.
Also see 'Dailc' as in 'Dhealc fhir sea é = fear ana-láidir, ana
gharbh' – a very strong man, a very rough man. Ó Briain.
'Dawk' – to drive a sharp instrument into anything; a sharp
pick, dig or stab. Wright.

DANTI-DAN !
An exclamation used by young boys in imitation of the sound
of horses' hoofs, usually used when coming out of cinemas
after seeing cowboy films. It was accompanied by one hand
striking the backside while the other hand was held in front of
the body as if it were holding a set of reins. It was said in a
sing-song repetitive manner – 'Danti-dan, danti-dan, danti-
dan, etc.'.
Derivation unknown.

DAW, noun
Fool, trifling matter.
Always used in negative context.
Use: He's no daw ! =
He's no fool.
Derivation: Probably Irish 'Dóigh'. 'Ní h-aon dóigh an fear
sin' – that man is not to be trifled with. Ó Domhnaill.
Also 'Dáe' – a human being. Meyer.

DAWN, BROWN, noun
Soft brown sugar.
Derivation unknown.

DAZA, ME, noun
Very pleasant.
Use: It's me daza =
    It's very nice.
Derivation: Possibly Irish 'Deas' – nice. Dinneen.
or 'Dessa' – right, just. Meyer.

DEAD MAN, noun
A term employed in a public-house to indicate that an empty
or partially-filled glass is no longer being used by a customer.
Use: They (the glasses) are dead men =
    The glasses are not being used.
Derivation: Old English. Partridge.
and note 'Empty bottles . . . . when the bottle is empty the
spirit is departed'. Brewer.

DEAD MAN, noun
A collector of life insurance.
Use: The dead man is coming =
    The insurance man is coming.
Derivation: All weekly-paid policies (particularly from the
Royal Liver Friendly Society) were taken out to pay the cost
of a funeral, hence 'Dead man' – the collector of the insurance
premiums.

DEKKO or DEKHO, noun

A look, a glance.

Use: Take a dekko at that =
Take a look at that.

Derivation: Possibly Irish 'D'fhéach' – past tense of 'Féach' to look.

Also 'Có-déicsiú' – a viewing together, and 'Déccain' – a seeing, a look. Meyer.

Possibly Hindustani 'Dekho' – to see. Concise Oxford Dictionary.

Note 'Dekho' probably introduced to Cork by the Munster Fusiliers.

a Dekko

DIDLUM, noun

A savings scheme. A group of people contribute an agreed amount of money over a fixed period of time. The money was not distributed until all of it was collected at the end of the period. Contrast with 'Manage' (which see).

Derivation unknown.

DIG, noun

A taunt.

Use: I see you had an old dig at him =
  I see you were taunting him.

Derivation: Unknown, but note 'Díg altas' and 'Díg laid' – vengeance, avenge. Meyer.

Possibly figurative use of 'to dig' as 'to poke' (a person in the ribs).

DIG, noun

A blow of the fist.

Use: He gave him a dig =
  He hit him with his fist.

Derivation: Probably 19th century – a straight left. Partridge.

See also 'Dig' above.

DINGER, noun

Excellence (used in adjectival phrase).

Use: He's a dinger of a player =
  He's a great player.

Derivation: Irish 'Dingim' – Bhíos bruite dingthe aige – he had crushed me and made me powerless to move. Dinneen.

'Dinge' – crushing, quelling, oppressing. Meyer.

Short for 'Humdinger' – anything excellent. Australian since 1920. Partridge.

DOG, BLACK, noun

An unpaid credit or slate (see).

Use: He left a black dog after him =
He left an unpaid bill (a slate) after him.

Derivation: Possibly 1705 counterfeit silver coin, hence 'Black Dog', and see 'Almost all of them had a 'black dog' somewhere'. Murphy.

DOLLOP, noun

Large measure (of whiskey or cream).

Use: He poured out two fine dollops of whiskey =
He poured out two large glasses of whiskey.

Derivation: Doubtful, but note 'Dáilead' – to pour out (especially drink at a festival). Marstrander.

and 'Dollop' – a lump, a large piece of something. Wright.

DON, noun

A card game played by 2, 4, 6 or 8 people, either singly or as partners, most often by 4 people. 13 cards each person and each entitled to nominate trumps in turn.

Scoring: Maximum 80, comprised of, 5 of any suit counts as 5, 5 of trumps counts as 10 and known as 'Small Don'.

9 of any suit counts as 9,

9 of trumps counts as 18 and called 'Big Don'.

Ace, King, Queen, Jack of Trumps count as 4, 3, 2 and 1 respectively.

Individual or partners to reach 80 first wins game.

DON, SMALL, noun

5 of trumps in game of 'Don' (see) counts double 10.

DON, BIG, noun

9 of trumps as in game of 'Don' counts double. See 'Don'.

DONKEY'S GUDGE, noun

A cake baked from the remnants of previous day's unsold cakes with a layer of pastry on top and at bottom. Dublin 'Gurcake', England 'Chester cake'. Derivation unknown.

DONKEY'S WEDDING CAKE, noun

As above with the addition of cream on top.

DOOSHIE, adjective

Small and neat.

Use: She's a dooshie little thing =
She's a lovely tidy little thing.

Derivation: Possibly Irish 'Duais' – a reward, a present, a dowry. Ó Domhnaill.

DOWTCHA BOY!

An expression of praise or acclaim, as at a game when a player distinguishes himself. 'Dowtcha boy!'

Derivation: Probably contraction of comment 'I don't doubt you, boy'.

DRAG or DRAGHUNT, noun
A cross-country dog race of about ten miles distance. The dogs are harriers, akin to foxhounds. Before the race, men lay a scent using meat or aniseed along the trail from the finishing point to the start, the hounds following the trail. The first dog to reach the finish is the winner.

Derivation: 'Drag' – a trail or scent, possibly a corruption of draw. Concise Oxford Dictionary.

and usual meaning 'to drag the meat across the countryside'.

DRAG, TO RUN A . . . . WITH
To have an unpleasant body odour.

Use: You could run a drag with that fellow =
There is a dreadful smell from that fellow.

Derivation: See 'Drag'.

DRAG, verb
To defeat, to overcome (sporting context).

Use: He ran a drag with the back =
He was far superior to the defender.

Derivation: See 'Drag' above.

DRISHEEN, noun
Type of sausage made from pigs' blood and tansey, recommended for invalids.

Derivation: Irish 'Drisín' – the main intestine of animals (such as sheep, goats, etc.) usually filled with foodstuff and cooked as pudding. Dinneen.

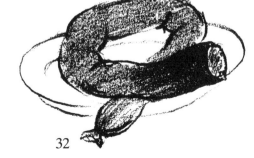

DROP, noun

A half measure of whiskey.

Derivation: Probably extension of drop – small quantity – but should not be taken literally when pouring out whiskey !

DROP, BAD, noun

Bad breeding, innate wickedness.

Use: There's a bad drop in that fellow =
He is wicked by nature.

Derivation: Unknown, but probably full phrase 'drop of blood'.

DROPSY, noun

A tip, a small favour.

Use: Did you get any dropsy ? =
Did you get a tip ?

Derivation: Possibly English 'Dropsy – bribery'. Partridge.

DUCK, noun

Loaf of bread of a distinctive shape.

Derivation unknown.

DUST, verb

To defeat, to overcome.

Use: I dusted him in the game =
I was superior to him in the game.

Derivation: Probably extension of meaning of dust, as throw dust in the eyes of, mislead, hence be superior.

also 'a bout or contest'. Wright.

I'll dust your jacket for you – I'll give you a good beating.

The allusion is to dusting carpets, etc. by beating them with a stick. Brewer.

and see 'Dust' – 'The piccolo tune was me dust' – favourite. Kelleher.

DUST, noun

The trade of stone-cutters.

Derivation: Dust from stone-cutting operations. See Murphy.

FAKIN, verb

To fish illegally with nets (usually for salmon).

Use: They were fakin last night =
They were fishing illegally last night.

Derivation: Unknown, but note 'to fake' – to cheat or swindle. Brewer.

FAST-ONE, TO PULL A, noun

To cheat.

Use: He pulled a fast-one on me =
He tricked me.

Derivation: Possibly from the game 'Fast and Loose' – a cheating game practised at fairs, the dupe being invited to put a stick in the loop of a coiled belt so that it cannot be pulled away, hence 'to play fast and loose' – to be shifty. Chambers.

FECK, noun

A game. 'Pitch and Toss'. '2-Up' (Australian).

Coins are thrown at a jack (which see). The person whose coin is nearest the jack is afforded the first opportunity to toss the coins. Should they come up 'heads' he keeps them, if 'harps' (or tails) the next man in line tosses and so on until all the coins have been 'headed' and retained. The game then recommences. Bets may also be made on each toss (which see).

Derivation unknown.

FECKING AROUND (WITH)
Playing around with, being inconclusive about something.
Use: He has been fecking around with that project for years =
He has been toying with that project for years.
Derivation unknown.

FLAH, noun and verb
Sexual intercourse, to have sexual intercourse.
Use: I had a great flah last night =
I enjoyed intercourse last night.
Derivation: Possibly Irish 'Fleadh' – party.
Note 'Fele' (Fíal) – that which causes shame, nakedness, pudenda.
Note 'Fell Óg' – a false virgin. Joynt and Knott.
Possibly corruption of Old Irish 'Sleith' – act of surprising a sleeping woman, having intercourse with her. Quin.
English 'Flay' – to criticise, to plunder (a person).
Old English 'Fléan', Middle Dutch 'Vlae', Old Norse 'Flá', from Germanic 'Flahan'. Compact English Dictionary.

FLAH-BAG, noun
A woman of loose virtue.
Use: She's an old flah-bag =
She is promiscuous.
Derivation: See 'Flah'.

FLAHED-OUT, adjective
Tired, exhausted.
Use: I'm flahed-out =
I'm exhausted.
Derivation: See 'Flah'.

FLAKE, noun and verb
A blow of a fist, to strike.
Use: I gave him a flake =
I struck him.
Derivation unknown.
Note "An' the terrier hauled off and made a flake at him".
Murphy.

FLY, adjective
Sneaky, devious.
Use: He's a fly boy =
He's cute, sneaky.
Derivation unknown.

FLY, verb
Aware of, conscious of.
Use: "I'm fly for that", said the foreman =
I'm aware of that. Murphy.
Derivation unknown.

FOODER, noun
Excitement, hurry.
Use: He's in an awful fooder =
He's in a high state of excitement.
Derivation: Irish 'Fuadar' – presage, haste, activity. Dinneen.
'Le Fúadar' – haste, hurry, eagerness. Joynt and Knott.

FOOSTER, noun

In a hurry, anxiety, fuss, agitation (used in adjectival phrase).

Use: He was all a fooster over the arrangements =
He was excited and hurried about the arrangements.

Derivation: Irish 'Fúster' – fussiness, immediate haste. Dinneen.

And note 'Perhaps our word is the result of confusing 'Fuadar' (see) – haste, activity, with 'Fuarcal' – panic, terror, and Cornish 'Fouster' – to bustle, to fuss about in a futile purposeless way'. Ó h-Éaluithe.

FOXER, noun

A job done by a tradesman in his spare time on contract to someone other than his normal employer (see 'Nixer').

Use: I did a foxer in wiring his house =
I wired his house after working hours.

Derivation: Note Irish 'Fochrach' – a hireling, a mercenary and 'Fochraic' – a reward, recompense, payment. Joynt and Knott.

FUNT, noun and verb

A kick (usually to a person's backside), to kick.

Use: He gave the young fellow a funt =
He gave the young lad a kick.

Derivation unknown.

GALLON, noun

A tin mug (usually of one-pint capacity).

Derivation: Irish 'Galún' – a gallon measure. Dinneen. See 'Gallon'.

Old Northern French 'Galon'. Oxford Concise Dictionary.

GALLON (TO GET ONE'S)

To be made redundant in the building (especially stone-masons) trade.

Use: He got his gallon last night =
He was made redundant last night.

Derivation: Unknown, possibly due to the fact that all workers carried their gallons (which see) with them from job to job. Hence 'to get one's gallon' – to be leaving the job.

'I hear that six stonies (stone-masons) got their gallon in Aherns last week'. Murphy.

GANDER, noun

A look, an inspection.

Use: Have a gander at that ! =
Have a look at that !

Derivation: 'Gander' (slang) – look, glance, Old English 'Gandra', Middle Low German, Dutch 'Gauder'. Concise Oxford Dictionary.

'Gander' – a long-necked bird, hence look. Partridge.

GASH, noun
Sex, sexual activity.
Use: She's a fine bit of gash =
She's a very sexy person.
Derivation: Irish 'Cais' – love, 'Caise' – passion. Dinneen.
The female pudend. Partridge.

GÁTCH, noun
A swagger, a distinctive gait (of a person).
Use: He has a right gatch on him =
He has a distinctive way of moving.
Derivation: Probably Irish 'Gáitse' – a showy gesture. Dinneen.
and 'Gaatch' (aa long as in car) – an affected gesture or movement of limbs, body or face. Joyce.
and cf. English 'Gait'. Ó h-Éaluithe.
and note spelt 'Gache'. Murphy.

GATTLE, verb
To chase girls with sexual motive.
Use: We were gattling last night =
We were chasing girls last night.
Derivation unknown.

GAUZER, noun
An attractive girl.
Use: She's a gauzer =
She is very attractive.
Derivation: Possibly from wearing gauze, thus decorative, attractive.

GAWK, verb and noun

To stare, a look, a glance.

Use: Have a gawk at that =
Have a look at that.

Derivation unknown.

GAWK, noun and verb

Vomit, to vomit (generally as a result of having had too much to drink).

Use: He gawked his heart out =
He was very sick.

Derivation: Unknown, but not 'to hawk or spit'. Wright.
May be a corruption of 'Hawk'.

GAZA, noun

Public gas lamp.
See 'Wax'.

GEANC, noun

A snub nose.

Use: She has a geanc of a nose =
She has a snub nose.

Derivation: Irish 'Geannc' – a snub nose. Dinneen.
'Genc' – a snub nose, a snub-nosed animal. Byrne.

GEE-UP, noun

Badinage, light raillery, a slag (which see).

Use: He gave him a right gee-up =
He mocked him unmercifully.

Derivation unknown.

GIDDUM, noun

Ardour, high spirits.

Use: He has a lot of giddum in him today =
He is full of life today.

Derivation: Irish 'Giodam' – restlessness, liveliness, giddi-ness. Dinneen.

GLASSEY ALLEY, noun

A large glass marble used in game of marbles (which see).

Derivation: 'Game of marbles – a glassey-alley being prized'. Partridge.

GLAWM, noun and verb

A rough caress, to grab, to snatch, to fondle roughly (sexual connotations).

Use: He made a glawm at her =
He grabbed at her.

Derivation: Irish 'Glám' – to grasp, to clutch. Dinneen.

And note 'to grasp, to clutch at, to snatch' (Ireland, Scotland, Cumbria). Wright.

GLIGEEN, noun

An empty-headed individual, a person who talks too much.

Use: He's a gligeen =
He is a giddy person.

Derivation: Irish 'Gligín' – a babbler, hence as above. Dinneen.

GOBBLE-JOB, noun
Fellatio.

Use: She gave him a gobble-job last night =
She practised fellatio on him last night.

Derivation: Local corruption of extension in meaning of gobble.
and English 'to eat hurriedly and noisily'. Concise Oxford Dictionary.

GOBS, GAME OF, noun
A game with five stones played by children – 'by throwing them up and catching them as they fall'. Joyce.
Derivation unknown.

GOBS, MOUTHFUL OF,
A person with large teeth.
Derivation: Probably Irish 'Gob' – mouth. Dinneen.

GOM, noun
Foolish person.

Use: He's an awful gom =
He's a very foolish person.

Derivation: See 'Amal' or 'Gamal' – a simpleton, a stupid-looking fellow. Dinneen.

GONONSTRIPS, noun
Instructions – details of routine.

Use: It's his job to give all the new workers the gonon strips =
It's his job to explain the routine to the new workers.

Derivation: Unknown, but probably corruption of 'to be going on with' *i.e.* proceeding.

GOOSAH, TO PLAY, verb
To act as chaperon.
Use: 'Playing goosah'.
Derivation: Probably diminutive of gooseberry.

GOWL, noun
The female pudenda.
Derivation: Irish 'Gabhal' – fork, groin, pelvis. Dinneen.
'Gabal' – 'Gabbal' – a fork, the fork of the body, the thighs.
Byrne.

GOWL, noun
A fool, an unpleasant individual.
Use: Don't be doing the gowl =
Don't be acting the fool.
Derivation: See 'Gowl' above and also note 'Goll', 'Caoch' –
blind, a perversion of Irish 'Dall' – blind. Bog Latin,
MacAlister.

GRASS, verb
To whip (spinning top).
Use: Grass the top for me =
Whip the top for me (get it to spin on its end).
Derivation: Irish 'Greas' – a turn (at a game) and 'Greasaim'
– I beat, I strike, hence to beat the top with the lash of the
whip. Dinneen.
and 'Gres' – an attack, a hostile encounter. 'Na trí fhuargres –
of the three cold strokes'. Byrne.

GRIG, verb
To tempt, to tantalise (especially in relation to children). Hence – Don't be grigging the child (by, for instance, offering sweets but withdrawing them as the child reaches for them). Derivation: From Irish 'Griogadh'. 'Na bí ag déanamh griogtha ar an leanbh leis – Don't be tempting (grigging) the child with it'. Dinneen.

GUINER, noun
A hurler who holds the hurley right hand below left while playing off his right side, awkward. See 'Ciotóg'. Derivation unknown.

GULLY, noun
All a bah ! (which see).
Use: All a gully =
All a bah !.
Derivation unknown.

GURREY, noun
Steering car. See 'Steerinah'.
Derivation: Unknown, but note 'a hand barrow' (Devon and Cornwall). Wright.

GUTTY (BOY), noun
A most undesirable person.
Use: He's a gutty (boy) =
He is an uncouth individual.
Derivation: Possibly Irish 'Gotaire' – a goatish individual. Dinneen.
See 'Gutter' – a place of low breeding or vulgar behaviour. Concise Oxford Dictionary.

GUZZ-EYE, noun

A 'cast' in an eye, a slight squint.
See 'Scoot'.
Derivation unknown.

GUZZLE, noun

A party, social gathering.
Use: I was at a guzzle last night =
I was at a party last night.
Derivation: Doubtful, but note 'Guzzle' – to eat, drink hurriedly, hence party. (Perhaps Old French 'Gossiller' – chatter, vomit) (Gossier – throat). Concise Oxford Dictionary.

GWALL, noun

A load, a large quantity or amount.
Use: He had a gwall of them =
He had a large quantity of them.
Derivation: Irish 'Gábháil' – 'as much as can be taken between the outstretched hands'. Dinneen.

H.L.I.!

Coward, cowardice (usually heard at soccer games). Contemptuous exclamation directed at a player.
Use: H.L.I.! =
Coward!
also *He has a touch of the Higos*
and *He has the Higo Shytes =*
He is cowardly.
Derivation: Initial letters of Highland Light Infantry, a British regiment despised by Cork people and not known for their bravery. See 'Sawney'.

HACK, noun

Fun, gaiety.

Use: We had great hack at the hooley =
We had great fun at the party.

Derivation: Unknown, but note 'to play hack – to frolic' (Suffolk). Wright.

HASTENER, noun

A form of draughter used to help a fire (household) ignite.

Use: Put the hastener to the fire, it's going out =
Put the hastener against the open fire to help it catch fire.

Derivation: Probably 'Hasten' – to quicken. The hastener usually consisted of a sheet of tin, large enough to cover the opening of an 'open' fire, the air was sucked into the fire through the grate. It was a primitive form of bellows. Sheets of newspaper were also used in similar fashion.

And note 'a semi-circular screen lined with tin placed behind meat roasting before the fire to keep cold air off and hasten cooking by reflected heat' (many English counties). Wright.

HALF, FINE, noun

Pretty girl.

Use: His sister is a fine half =
His sister is a beautiful girl.

Derivation unknown.

HANGING, adjective and adverb

Drunk (also used for emphasis).

Use: He is hanging drunk =
He is very drunk.

Derivation unknown.

HEAP, TO BE UP IN A,
To be confused, disorganised.
Use: The politicians are up in a heap during economic
recessions =
The politicians are confused during economic recessions.
Derivation unknown.

HIGOS, A TOUCH OF THE, noun
See 'H.L.I.'

HIGO SHYTES
See 'H.L.I.'

HISE, verb
To lift up, to hoist.
Use: The jockey was hised up on the horse =
The jockey was given a leg-up on the horse.
Derivation: Probably a corruption of hoist.
And note ' . . . . they caught the job as if 'twas a sack of
meal and hised it into position'. Murphy.

HOBBLE, noun and verb
Theft, to steal.
Use: He hobbled the parts he needed to repair the car =
He stole the parts he needed to repair the car.
also
He did a hobble =
He stole.
Derivation unknown.

HOOFLER, noun and verb
A trickster.
Use: He is a hoofler =
He is a trickster.
Derivation unknown.
And note 'The biggest hoofler I ever worked with'. Murphy.

HOP, ON THE, noun
Absent without permission from school.
See 'Lang'.
Derivation: Obscure, but note 'Hop' – 'enjoying oneself'.
Partridge.

HOP OFF!, verb
Go away !
Use: Go on and hop off ! =
Go away !
Derivation unknown.

HOP, A . . . OFF, TO HAVE, verb
To tease.
Use: I had a hop off him =
I teased him.
also *I hopped off him.*
Derivation unknown.

ÍRE, noun
Anger, excitement.
Use: His ire is up =
He is angry.
Derivation: Irish 'Irach' – wrathful, quick to anger. O'Daly
and O'Sullivan.
And note Latin 'Ira' – anger. Concise Oxford Dictionary.

IRE, noun
Windgall, chafing on legs.
Use: The poor child has ire on his thighs =
The poor child's legs are chafed.
He suffers from windgall.
Derivation: Irish 'Oighear' meaning friction, windgall.
'Tá oighear ar mo chois – my leg is chafed'. Dinneen.

IRE, TOUCH OF, noun
Sexual arousal.
Use: I have a touch of ire =
I am sexually aroused.
Derivation: Possibly the Irish 'Oighear' (see 'Ire') – heat of
the blood, hence arousal. Dinneen.

JACK, noun
A sexual erection.
Derivation: Possibly from 'Jack' – an implement to lift
weights. To rise up, hence an erection.

JAG, noun and verb
An appointment with a member of the opposite sex.
Use: He has a jag with that girl tonight =
He has an appointment with that girl tonight.
Derivation unknown.

JIBBER, noun and verb
A coward, to jib.
Use: There was never a jibber in our family =
There was never a coward in our family.
Derivation: 'Jibber' – refuse to proceed in some action,
hence to show cowardice (19th century, origin unknown).
Concise Oxford Dictionary.
Probably 19th century English verb 'Jib' – to shirk. Partridge.

JOCKEY, noun

Coin resting on 'Jack' in game of 'Feck' (which see).
Derivation: Probably from 'Jockey' as a person who rides on top of a horse.

JOLLY, noun

A favourite in a dog or horse race.
Use: The jolly is at two to one =
The favourite is priced at two to one.
Derivation: Unknown, but note French 'Le joli de la chose c'est que' – 'the best of the thing is on'. Cassells.

JORUM, noun

A drink (of alcohol).
Use: Have a jorum ! =
Have a drink.
Derivation: 'Jorum' – large drinking bowl, perhaps from jorum. Concise Oxford Dictionary.
'Shelta' – yorum, milk, hence a drink. MacAlister.
'Jorum' – a drinking bowl (a large wine jar). Partridge.

JOULTER, exclamation

A form of nickname (used only in a derogatory fashion when calling a person).
Use: Hey, joulter ! =
Hey, you !
Derivation: Difficult, but note Irish 'Seoltóir' – a jolter or jobber. Seoltóir éisc – a fish-jobber. Dinneen.
Irish 'Seoltóir' – a drover and 'Seoltóir bó' – a cattle-drover. Ó Domhnaill.
And 'Jolter-head' – a stupid person, a blockhead, an idiot (many English counties). Wright.

JUB-JUBS, noun
A jelly sweet.
Derivation: Probably corruption of 'Jujube' – lozenge of gelatin flavoured with edible berry-like drupe of certain plants, sold in chemists as a remedy for cough.
French or Medieval Latin, possible origin Greek 'Zizuphon'. Concise Oxford Dictionary.

KARROGE, noun
A cockroach, a beetle.
Derivation: Irish 'Cíaróg' – cockroach, beetle. Dinneen.

KICK, noun
Sixpence.
Use: I have two and a kick =
I have two shillings and sixpence (half-a-crown).
17th century coin of sixpence value. Partridge.
And Anglo-Saxon 'Cicle' – a bit. Brewer.
In Jamaica, a 'Bit' equals sixpence.

KICK, noun and verb
To request a favour (a job or loan).
Use: I kicked him for a job =
I asked him for a job.
Derivation: Kick for trade – as for a job (tailors) from 1855. Partridge.
Note ' . . . . kick him for a rise next week'. Murphy.

KILTER, OUT OF
Out of place, out of line.
Use: The machine is gone out of kilter =
The machine is not working properly.
Out of good working order.
Derivation: 17th century, origin unknown. Concise Oxford Dictionary.

KISSER, noun

Face.

Use: I broke his kisser with a clout =
I broke his face with a blow.

Derivation: 'Kisser' (slang) – face, mouth. Concise Oxford Dictionary.

Unknown, but probably from association with 'kiss'. Note the 'mouth'. Partridge.

KNACKER, noun

A trickster, a disreputable individual (usually with reference to tinkers).

Use: Don't trust him, he's a knacker =
Don't trust him, he's a trickster.

Derivation: Note Irish 'Bitheamhnach' – a thief, a rascal. Dinneen.

Note 'Shelta' – naker, a tinker. MacAllister.

KNAWVSHAWLING

Quarrelling, finding fault with.

Use: He's always knawvshawling =
He's always quarrelling.

Derivation: Irish 'Cnáimhseáil' – act of complaining, grumbling. Dinneen.

And see 'Knauvshauling' – grumbling, Irish 'Cnámh' – a bone, the jaw-bone. Joyce

KYBOSH, noun

To put an end to something, to terminate or stymie.

Use: 'This will put the kybosh on everything ='
This will put an end to everything (scheme, etc.). Murphy.

Derivation: Irish 'Caidhp Báis' – the death cap, hence an end and note spelling. Ó h-Éaluithe.

Note Irish 'Caidhp' – a coif. Dinneen.

and 'Caidhp Bás' – death cap (botany). Ó Domhnaill.

and 'Kibosh' – nonsense, put an end to, finally dispose of (19th century, origin unknown). Concise Oxford Dictionary.

and 'Kybosh' – some sort of difficulty or 'fix'. 'He put the kybosh on him – he defeated him'. Joyce.

'Kibosh' as above (military, First World War, Put the kibosh on the Kaiser). Perhaps Yiddish 'Kyebosh' or 'Kibosh' – eighteen pence. Partridge.

and note 'Kybosh' – wages, money (Cornwall). Wright.

and see 'The woman had put the kibosh on things with her dastardly threats'. O'Mahony.

LACE, noun

A blow.

Use: I gave him a lace =
I struck him.

Derivation: Irish 'Léasaim' – I beat violently, whip, lacerate. Dinneen.

and cf. English 'Lace' – to whip. Ó h-Éaluithe.

and 'Lace' – to thrash, to flog (obscure). Partridge.

LAG, verb

To hold on to the tailboard of a moving vehicle.

Use: He was lagging behind the lorry but fell off and was hurt =
He was holding on to the tailboard of the lorry but fell off
and was hurt.

Derivation: Unknown, but note English 'Lag' – to fall behind, hence stay behind. Concise Oxford Dictionary.

But note 'Scut the whip' (Dublin). Eilis Brady.

On the Lang

LAMP, verb

To watch, to look at, to see.

Use: He's always lamping the women =
He's always watching the women.

Derivation: Probably extension of 'to lamp' – to illuminate, hence see.

LAND, noun

A disappointment.

Use: He got an awful land when he didn't get the job =
He was very disappointed when he didn't get the job.

Derivation unknown.

LANG, ON THE, noun and verb

Absence from school without permission or valid reason (to mitch).

Use: I was on the lang yesterday =
I was on the hop (see) yesterday.

Derivation unknown.

LANGER, noun

A disagreeable person.

Use: Go away, you langer =
Go away, you fool.

Derivation: Unknown, but note 'Élang' – defect, flaw, weak spot. Joynt and Knott.

LANGER, noun

A penis.

Derivation: Unknown, but 'Langur' – a long-tailed monkey from India. Concise Oxford Dictionary.

Note influence of the Munster Fusiliers.

LANGERS, adjective and adverb.
Drunk. Also used for emphasis, *e.g.* langers drunk – very drunk.
Use: He was langers again last night =
He was drunk again last night.
Derivation unknown.

LASH, noun

A blow.

*Use: I gave him a lash in the kisser =
I struck him in the face.*

Derivation: Irish 'Lais' – a lash. Dinneen.

Béarlagar na saer – lash a hand'. MacAlister.

'Lash' – strike violently. Possibly Low German Origin. Concise Oxford Dictionary.

LASH, noun

A very attractive girl.

*Use: She's a lash =
She is very attractive.*

Derivation: Possibly Irish 'Laise' or 'Luise' – glamour. Dinneen.

LASH-UP, noun

Hearty meal.

*Use: We had a great lash-up after the match =
We had a grand meal after the match.*

Derivation unknown.

LASHER, A very attractive girl.

See 'Lash'.

LEDDER, verb

To beat severely (usually with some implement).

Use: I leddered him =
I gave him a severe beating.

Derivation: Possibly Irish 'Leadaráil – act of lashing, Dinneen.

or possibly a corruption of 'Leather' – a leather strap used to punish pupils at school.

But note 'Leather' – to beat. This is not derived as might be supposed from the English word leather (tanned skin), but from the Irish in which it is of very old standing: 'Letrad' (modern 'Leadradh') – cutting, hacking, lacerating, also a champion fighter, a warrior, a leatherer. (Corm. Gloss, 9th century). Joyce.

'Ledder' probably a corruption of a heavy blow. Wright.

Note 'Leadradh' – striking, tearing, cutting, dissecting, whipping, destroying. Dinneen.

and 'Leadradh' – a thrashing and 'Leadradh a fháil – to get a leathering'. Ó Domhnaill.

and 'Leather' – to beat, thrash. Partridge.

LEVIT, noun

A blow with the fist.

Use: He gave him a levit =
He struck him with his fist.

Derivation unknown.

LICK UP TO, verb

To fawn on.

Use: He licks up to his superiors =
He fawns on his superiors.

Derivation unknown.

LICK, or LICK INTO A FIT, verb

To defeat, to surpass, to overcome.

Use: Cork licked Tipperary into a fit =
Cork defeated Tipperary easily.

Derivation: Possibly 19th English. Lick and also lick into fits. Partridge.

and note 'Lick' – a blow, a stroke, a cut with a sword. Wright.

LINE, DOING A

Keeping company.

Use: He's doing a line =
He is keeping company.

Derivation: Possibly French 'Ligner' – to copulate. Concise Oxford Dictionary.

'Be lined' (1909) – to be married (generally of women). Partridge.

A marriage certificate, the banns of a marriage. Wright.

LIP, TO HAVE A . . . FOR, noun

To have a great desire for (usually drink).

Use: He has a great lip on him for drink =
He has a great liking for alcoholic drink.

Derivation: Doubtful, but probably related to 'Lip', hence taste and appetite.

and note 'to taste'. Wright.

LIP, TO HAVE A . . . ON, verb

To be upset, annoyed, peeved, to pout.

Use: He'll have a lip on him now that you won't give him what he wants =
He'll be annoyed now that you won't give him what he wants.

Derivation: Doubtful, but probably related to 'Lip' – pouting in annoyance.

'He'd have a lip on him if he'd have to wait'. Murphy.

LOP, noun

A penny.

Use: Give the child a lop =
Give the child a penny.

Derivation unknown.

LOSSET, noun

Table, trestle tables used by dealers on Coal Quay to display fruit, vegetables, etc.

Derivation: Irish 'Losad' – a kneading trough, figuratively a table spread with food. Dinneen.

A kneading tray for making cakes. Joyce.

A large flat wooden dish. Wright.

Also note Irish 'Last' – a large quantity or lot of anything, hence a lot of goods on display and 'lossets'. Dinneen.

LOWRY, noun

A blow of a fist.

Use: He got a lowry into the puss =
He was struck with the fist in the face.

Derivation: Possibly Irish 'Ladhar' – a handful. Dinneen.

'Ladhar' – 'Lán mo ladhar – fistful'. Ó Briain.

'Lober' (Lobra), 'Shelta' – to hit, strike. MacAlister.

MÁLA, noun

A type of modelling plasticine (especially used by children in school).

Derivation: Probably Irish 'Márla' – marl, a kind of rich clay, 'Márla buí' – yellow subsoil of a plastic consistency. Dinneen.

Also 'Márla' – clay, romance loan word. Joynt.

Note 'Shelta', 'Mála' – a hand or to handle. MacAlister.

MANKY, adjective

Dirty, filthy.

Use: His hair was manky (with the dirt) =
His hair was very dirty.

Derivation: Possibly Irish 'Mongach' – maned, long-haired. Dinneen.

'Mongach' – long-haired, hairy. Joynt.

See 'Mankie' – rotten, very inferior. Possibly from French 'Manqué'. Partridge.

MANAGE, noun

A savings scheme operated over a given period of time by a fixed number of people contributing a pre-determined amount of money each week. The members drew lots to decide the order of drawing the collection – but the organiser had the option of taking the first collection. Manages were considered a bad risk as members who collected in the early weeks of the scheme were known to default, leaving the other members short of money. Contrast with 'Didlum' (which see).

Derivation unknown.

MARK, noun

A person who is likely to accede to a request for a loan of money.

Use: He's an easy mark =
He usually gives money easily.

Derivation: Irish 'Marc' – 'Is maith an marc leis an airgead é – he is good surety for the money'. Dinneen.

Possibly from a sign used by tramps to denote a good giver.

MASHER, noun

Good-looking man.

Use: He's a masher =
He's very attractive.

Derivation: Irish 'Maise' – beauty, 'Maiseach' – beauty, well-dressed, decorated. Dinneen.

'Maise' – goodliness, comeliness, fineness. Joynt.

and 'Maiseach' – dress elegantly.

and 'Deg-maiseach' – very beautiful. Marstrander.

and 'Masher' – an exquisite, a lardy-dardy swell who dresses aesthetically (1880). Brewer.

MASSIVE, adjective

Very attractive.

Use: Mary, your dress is massive =
Mary, your dress is lovely.

Derivation: Old Irish 'Mass' – excellence of appearance or external quality, commonly of persons – fine, handsome. Joynt.

MAUSER, noun

A big, fleshy woman (derogatory).

Use: She's a big mauser of a wan =
She's a big fleshy woman.

Derivation: Possibly Irish 'Más' – the buttocks, hip, thigh. Dinneen.

and Irish 'Másach' — having large buttocks. Joynt.

also 'Mauzy'. Ó hÉaluithe.

MAWKISH, adjective

Of unpleasant, indeterminate appearance, taste (food, drink), disagreeable, sentimental.

Use: The food was mawkish =
The food was unpleasant, somewhat tasteless.

Derivation: Irish 'Máchail' – stain, defect, fault, 'Gan máchail' – stainless, Latin 'Macula'. Dinneen.

'Mawkish' – of faint, sickly flavour, feebly sentimental, 'Mawk' (obsolete) – maggot, etc. Concise Oxford Dictionary.

'Mawkish' – slatternly (1720 – 70). Partridge.

'Mawkish' – insipid, sick from drink, slightly indisposed. Wright.

MEB, noun

A small glassy alley (which see) used in a game of marbles (see).

Derivation unknown.

MEBS, noun

A fool, a stupid person.

Use: Go away, you mebs =
Go away, you fool.

Derivation: Unknown, but note Irish 'Mebul' – a cause of shame, a disgrace. Joynt.

MEBS, noun

The testicles.

Use: He got a kick in the mebs =
He got a kick in the testicles.

Derivation: Unknown, but note 'Mebs' above – marbles, hence balls.

Note 'Bean mebla' – a harlot. Meyer.

MEEJUM, noun

Measure of stout. Probably a medium, somewhere between a half and a pint. Usually refers to half-pint (stout).

Derivation unknown.

MOCKEYAH
Not serious, not for real, in jest.
Use: I only said that mockeyah =
I only said that in jest.
Derivation: Unknown, but could be a corruption of Irish,
'Mar dheadh' – pretence, or influence of English 'to mock'.

MOCKEEN, noun
A spoiled child.
Use: He's a little mockeen =
He's a spoiled individual (he's saucy).
Derivation: Irish 'Maicín' – a pet, a spoiled child. Dinneen.

MOOLAH, noun
Money.
Use: I have no moolah =
I have no money.
Derivation: Note 'Mol' and 'Airgead na mholtraca agus na
mhaoiseogaibh – plenty of money'. Dinneen.
'Moolah' – money. Joyce.
Note 'Money' (20th century slang, origin unknown). Concise
Oxford Dictionary.

MORERAN
More than.
Use: He got moreran me =
He got more than me.
Derivation: Corruption of 'more than'.

MOYLOW, noun

Drunk, inebriated.

Use: He was moylow last night =
He was very drunk last night.

Derivation: Possibly corruption of Irish 'Maith go leór' literally meaning well enough, but in context meaning inebriated. 'Tá sé maith go leor – he is a bit tipsy'. Ó Domhnaill.

MUG, noun

A foolish person.

Use: Don't be a mug =
Don't be a fool.

Derivation: A male slave or servant, a fool, a simpleton (English Court). Wright.

'Mug' – simpleton, gullible person, probably from Scandinavian. Concise Oxford Dictionary.

MULLACKER, noun

A rough unskilled person (especially a hurler or a footballer).

Use: He's a mullacker =
He's rough, unskilled.

Derivation: Probably Irish 'Mullachán' – a sturdy, fairly big boy. Dinneen.

And note 'Mullock' (dating back to 1852) – an ignorant or otherwise worthless person. Partridge.

MUSIC, noun

The sound of harriers baying at a drag (see).

Derivation: The baying of the hounds is considered by the huntsmen to be as pleasant as music.

NAPPER, noun

Head, brain.

Use: He fell and split his napper =
He fell and cut his head.
also
Use your napper =
Think ! (literally use your head).
Derivation: Doubtful, but note 'Napachán' – a dull-witted person. Partridge.

NATIONAL, noun

Collection (money). Generally a collection for a charitable purpose to replace money when lost, to defray medical expenses, etc.

Use: We had a national for him to pay for his operation =
We had a collection for him to pay for his operation.
Derivation unknown.

NINER, noun

A card-game played by a maximum of five people, each player receiving nine cards, similar rules to three-card brag (see).

NOODEENAW, noun

A person of insipid or annoying character.

Use: He's a noodeenaw =
He's an insipid individual.
Derivation: Irish 'Niúdar neádar' – indecision, an undecided reply, and 'Bhí niúdar neádar aige – he was hesitating'. Dinneen.
and 'Niúdar neudar' – indistinct, grumbling, indistinct muttering of any sort. Ó Briain.

NOOKS, noun
Money.
Derivation: Shelta 'Nuk' – a penny.
'Nook' – a penny (especially vagrants). MacAlister.

ODDS, MILK AND, noun
Cakes, milk and cakes.
Use: We had milk and odds after training =
We had milk and cakes after training.
Derivation unknown.

ONE, noun
A word used in card games (three-card brag, niner, poker) to
describe a hand of the same suit (also called 'Blue'), hence an
'Ace-one' a hand of one suit, 'Ace-high'.
Derivation: Unknown, but probably because all cards are of
the same colour, hence all one.

OUT, TO BE HAD, verb
To be deceived.
Use: I was had out =
I was fooled.
Derivation: Unknown, but possibly literal translation of Irish
'Bheith amuigh ar – to be out with (to deceive)'.

OWNSHUCK, noun
A simple person.
Use: He's an old ownshuck =
He's a simple, harmless person.
Derivation: Irish 'Óinseach' – a fool (especially a female fool,
a giddy woman). Dinneen.

PARALATIC, adjective
Drunk, intoxicated.

Use: He's was paralatic =
He was drunk to a state of insensibility.

Derivation: Corruption of 'Paralytic' – incapable of movement.

PANA, DOING, verb
Walking up and down St. Patrick Street. A kind of Cork 'Paseo'.

PAVI, noun
A rough, uncouth individual, a tough.

Use: He's a pavi, that fellow =
That fellow is a tough.

Derivation unknown.

PAWNY, noun
Water or rain.

Use: The pawny is coming =
The rain is coming.

Derivation: Possibly Hindustani 'Pani' – water. Concise Oxford Dictionary. Probably brought to Cork by the Munster Fusiliers.

Shelta 'Pani' or 'Pawnee' – water from Romani. MacAlister.
Hindustani 'Pani' – water. Brewer.

PICKEY, noun
A street game played by children.

Use: We'll have a game of pickey =
We'll play pickey.

Derivation: Unknown, but also known as 'Hop-scotch' and 'Beds' or 'Pickey-beds' (Dublin). For a description of the game see Brady.
and 'Pickie' – the game of hop-scotch (Ireland). Wright.

Dickie

PITCH, verb

To throw coins at the 'Jack' in games of 'Feck', 'Skites' and 'Bee-up'.

Derivation: 'Pitch' – to throw, to fling. Concise Oxford Dictionary.

PIZAWN, noun

A small scrawny individual.

Use: He's a little pizawn =
   He is a scrawny little individual.

Derivation: Possibly Irish 'Píosa' – a child and 'Píosán' – a little bit. Dinneen

PLAIN, noun

A loaf of bread of distinctive shape, known elsewhere as 'Wellington'.
Derivation unknown.

PLANK, noun and verb

A hiding-place, to conceal.
Use: A plank of 'blackas' =
A secret place in which blackberries grow in profusion.
Derivation: Possibly pre-19th century English 'Plank' – to conceal. Partridge.

PLANK, verb

To bury.
Use: They planked him in the 'Pirana Gardens' this morning =
They buried him in St. Joseph's Graveyard (formerly the
Botanic Gardens) this morning.
Derivation: Possibly from 'Plank' above.

POLE, UP THE, adjective

Pregnant (usually with reference to an unmarried girl).
Use: His sister is up the pole =
His sister is pregnant.
Derivation: Note 'Up the pole' (slang) – in a fix. Concise Oxford Dictionary.

PONNEY, noun

An enamel or tin mug used extensively in primary schools when free milk was distributed to the pupils.
Derivation unknown.

PONTOON, noun

A card game also known as '21' and 'Black-jack'.
Derivation: Possibly a corruption of French 'Vingt et un' – twenty-one, a game of cards. Concise Oxford Dictionary.

POOLEY, noun

Urine.
Use: To do one's pooley =
   To urinate.
Derivation: Unknown, possibly a corruption of 'Fual' – urine. Dinneen.
and note 'Pooley' – urine (Ireland and West Cumbria). Wright.
and note ' . . . . When you lot were putting volumes of pooley through your mother's apron'. O'Mahony.

POXED, verb

Extremely lucky.
Use: He's poxed with luck =
   He's extremely lucky.
Derivation unknown.

PRIELL, noun

Term used in 'Niner' and 'Three-card Brag' (see) card games to describe a set of three cards of the same value, hence 'A priell of aces' – three aces.
Derivation unknown.

PUCK, verb

To stroke-haul (fish). An illegal method of fishing using three hooks bound together and used without bait. A form of gaffing.
Derivation unknown.

PUCK, verb and noun

A blow of the fist, to strike with the fist.
Use: I gave him a puck in the gob (see) =
I gave him a blow in the face.
Derivation: 'Poc' – a sharp sudden blow (in games).
Dinneen.

PUSS, noun

Pouting.
Use: He has a puss on him =
He's pouting.
Derivation: Irish 'Pus' – 'Chuir sé pus air féin – he pouted'.
Dinneen.
'Pus' – a lip (generally in a contemptuous sense). Joynt.

QUEER-HAWK, noun
Strange individual.
Use: He's a queer-hawk =
He is an unusual individual.
Derivation: Unknown, but note 'Queer' – counterfeit money,
hence false. Brewer.

RACK, noun
A hair comb.
Use: He carries a rack in his top pocket =
He carries a hair comb in his top pocket.
Derivation: Irish 'Raca' – a rack or comb. Dinneen.
'Rack' – fixed or movable frame or wooden or metal bars (for
holding fodder), hence rack. Concise Oxford Dictionary.
'A bone', hence a comb. Partridge.

RAKE, A, noun
A large number (of things, objects).
Use: He has a rake of songs =
He has a large collection of songs.
Derivation: Unknown, but probably 'to rake' – to collect,
draw together. Concise Oxford Dictionary.

RANKER, noun
Coward.
Use: He's a ranker =
He's a coward.
Derivation: Unknown, but probably cognate with 'Rank' –
loathesome, indecent, corrupt, hence coward. Concise Oxford
Dictionary.

RAZZ, verb

To tease, provoke, jeer at.

Use: He razzed the players =
He teased the players.

Derivation: Probably abbreviation of 'Raspberry' (slang). Concise Oxford Dictionary.
or see
'To jeer at someone' (Australian). Partridge.
And note 'Razzer' – to vex, enrage (South Lancashire). Wright.

RECK, verb and noun

Recognise or recognition (used in a negative context only).

Use: He didn't give him a reck = or
He didn't reck him =
He didn't recognise him.

Derivation: Teutonic, Old English 'Reccan' – to pay heed to. Concise Oxford Dictionary.
And note 'Reck' – to take heed of, care for, reward (Scotland, London, Yorkshire). Wright.

RIDER, noun

Coin which rests against 'Jack' in game of 'Feck' (which see). Derivation unknown.

ROTTO, noun

Intoxicated.

Use: He was rotto again last night =
He was drunk again last night.

Derivation unknown.

RUBBER DOLLIES, noun

Canvas shoes, plimsolls.

Use: Put on your rubber dollies =
Put on your canvas shoes.

Derivation unknown.

RUCTIONS, noun

Uproar.

Use: He caused ructions in the pub =
He caused trouble – noise in the bar.

Derivation: 'Ruchtacht' – groaning, rumbling. Dinneen.

'Ruchtach' – that which makes a 'Rucht' or sound of some kind. Joynt.

Note 'The Insurrection of 1798 which was commonly called the Ruction'. Joyce.

SAWNEY, noun

A foolish type of person.

Use: I'm no sawney =
I'm no fool.

Derivation: 'Sawney' – local version of Sandy, short for Alexander, a derisive nickname for a Scotsman, a simpleton, also foolish, foolishly sentimental. The Shorter Oxford English Dictionary.

'Sawney' – a stage Scotsman, hence a caricature, a foolish person. Bartley. See 'H.L.I.'.

'Sawney' – a fool (general use Ireland and England). Wright.

SCAULD, noun

Tea.

Use: I'll have a cup of scauld =
I'll have a cup of tea.

Derivation: Unknown, but note 'Scála' – a cup, a bowl. Dinneen.

or from the practice of 'Scalding' – pouring boiling water into the teapot before putting tea in the pot.

SCATTER, TO CUT A, verb

To dress well, to impress.

Use: He cut a great scatter =
He looked extremely well dressed.

Derivation unknown.

SCONCE, noun and verb

Use: Give me a sconce at that =
Give me a look at that.

Derivation: Unknown, but probably Old French 'Esconse' – lantern, hence 'to see'. Concise Oxford Dictionary.

SCOOT-EYE, noun

Cast in the eye.

Use: Very few people have scoot-eyes now =
Very few people have casts in their eyes now.

Derivation unknown.

SCORE, verb

To succeed in attracting the favours of a girl.

Use: I scored at the dance =
I took a girl home from the dance.

Derivation: Unknown, but probably association of scoring and winning.

And note 'Score' – a reckoning, to make a reckoning, so called from the custom of marking off 'runs' or 'lengths' in games by the score feet. Brewer.

SCOVE, noun

A walk.

Use: I went for a scove =
I went for a walk.

Derivation: Unknown, but note 'Scove' (Scotland and East Anglia) – to fly equably, to poise on the wing (of a bird). Wright.

SCRIP, noun

Membership, subscription (of a club).

Use: The scrip is collected every week =
The membership subscription is collected every week.

Derivation: Possibly contraction of subscription.

Note Irish 'Screpul', Latin 'Screpulus', in law (ancient laws of Ireland) a unit of value, also fee, contribute, tribute. Quin.

And note 'Scrip' (Scotland and Kent) – a bill. Wright.

SCUTTLING, verb

Smoking the butt-ends of cigarettes.

Derivation unknown.

SEPTIC, adjective

To be affected, vain.

Use: That one (usually female) is septic =
That girl is extremely affected.

Derivation: Unknown, but note 'Septic' – putrifying.

SHAM, noun

A person, a fellow.

Use: Who's that sham ? =
Who's that person ?

Derivation: Note Shelta 'Sam' – a boy, man, fellow. Mac-Alister.

and 'The beoir of a sham' – the girl/woman of the fellow. MacMahon.

SHAPER, noun

A conceited person.
Use: He's a shaper =
He's affected.
Derivation: Person considered as impressing the sight.
Concise Oxford Dictionary.

SHEEFRA, noun

A gossip, a precocious child, an unpleasant individual.
Derivation: Irish 'Siodhbhrad' or 'Síofra' – a mischievous
child. Dinneen.

SHELLITYHORN, noun

Snail.
Description of snail as in verse recited by children.
  'Shellity, shellity horn,
  Stick out your four black horns'.
Derivation: 'Seillide' – a snail. Quin.
Note 'Shelmidy'. Ó h-Éaluithe.

SHERANG, noun

A works foreman.

Use: The sherang will give you the gonon strips (see) =
The foreman will explain the routine.

Derivation unknown.

SHLOWNY, adjective

Slippery (surface or object).

Use: The hill (tray) is fierce shlowny =
The hill is very slippery.

Derivation: Irish 'Sleamhain' – smooth, sleek, slippery.
Dinneen.

and 'Slemda', 'Slemaigid' – smooth, slippery, makes smooth,
polishes. Quin, Joynt, Condon, O'Daly, O'Sullivan.

SHOWERY!

Cry of warning or alarm, warning shout.

Use: Showery! The guards are coming =
Watch out! The guards are coming.

Derivation unknown.

SKALP, verb

To cheat (of money).

Use: He'll skalp you if you're not careful =
He'll cheat you if you are not careful.

Derivation: 'Sceilpéir' – a rogue, a pickpocket. Dinneen.

SKELP, noun

A blow.

Use: He took a skelp out of him =
He struck him a blow.

Derivation: 'Scelp' – a splinter, a thorn. Quin.
'Scealp' – a splinter, a blow or slap. Note 'Not as ponderous as a clout'. Ó h-Ealuithe.
'I remember a stone-carver from Dublin who was always taking skelps off his knuckles'. Murphy.
'Skelp' (Ireland, Scotland, North and Midland Counties) – to strike with the hand or with a flat surface. Wright.

SKEOG, noun

A haw, the berry of the whitethorn.

Use: We were picking skeogs =
We were picking haws.

Derivation: Irish 'Sceachóg' – a small thorn bush, a haw. Dinneen.

SKEORY, noun

A haw, the berry of the whitethorn.

Use: We were picking skeories =
We were picking haws.

Derivation: Irish 'Sceachóir' – a haw, the fruit of the dog-rose.
But note 'Skeory', the latter meaning has never been heard of by the author, the fruit of the dog-rose is commonly known as hips, 'itchy-backs', 'jacky-dorys'. Ó h-Ealuithe.
Note 'Itchy-backs' – the seed of the haws or dog-roses was taken, a light fluffy irritant, and pushed down inside children's clothes to cause itchiness, hence 'itchy-backs'.

SKITE, noun

A drinking session.

Use: He was on a fierce skite =
He was on the batter (which see).

Derivation: Unknown, but note 'Skite' – a silly frivolous light-headed person. Joyce.

SKITES, noun

A game somewhat similar to 'Feck' but played with two coins and using two 'Jacks' (see). Points are awarded to the coins nearest the 'Jack'. Slates shaped into circular pieces were used when coins were not available.

Derivation unknown.

SKULL, noun

A loaf of bread of distinctive shape.

Derivation unknown.

SLAG, noun and verb

Badinage, ridicule, to mock, to make fun of.

Use: To slag someone =
To make fun of someone. To ridicule someone.

Derivation: Unknown, but possibly a corruption of the Irish 'Sleagach' – sneaking, drawling, sly. Dinneen.

SLATE, noun

To run up a bill (usually in a public-house).

Use: He has a slate in every pub in Cork =
He owes money in every pub in Cork.

Derivation: Unknown, but probably derived from the former practice of keeping records of amounts due by customers in public-houses and shops. Slates were used.

SLATES, AWAY FOR
To be happy, comfortable, satisfied.
Use: He's away for slates now that he has a job =
He's O.K. now that he has a job.
Derivation: Unknown, but possibly a corruption of slate, hence free of debt.

SLOB, noun
A harmless person, an easy-going individual.
Use: He's a poor old slob =
He's a nice, harmless individual.
Derivation: Possibly Irish 'Slob' – a soft-faced individual. Dinneen.

SLOCK (SLOCKING), verb
To steal apples from an orchard.
Use: To go slocking =
To take apples from an orchard.
Derivation: Possibly a corruption of 'Slog' – to steal apples. Partridge.

SLOG, noun
A blow (with the open hand).
Use: He gave him a slog across the face =
He struck him in the side of the face with the open hand.
Derivation: Possibly German 'Schlag' – a blow. Cassells.

SLUG, noun

A swallow (drink).

Use: I took a slug out of the bottle =
I took a drink out of the bottle.

Derivation: 'Slug' or 'Slugadh' – a sudden swallow, a gulp.
Dinneen.

A drink of unascertained kind of strong liquor. Partridge.

SMACK, noun

Liking, regard.

Use: I have a great smack for that fellow =
I like that fellow.

Derivation: Possibly 14th century English 'Smack' – enjoyment. Partridge.

SMATHERS, TO MAKE OF, verb

To defeat utterly.

Use: He made smathers of him =
He beat him in a fist fight.

Derivation: Irish 'Smeádar' – a heavy blow. Dinneen.

Note 'Smaadher' – to break into small pieces. Joyce.

SMUSH, noun

Face.

Use: I'll smash your smush =
I'll smash your face.

Derivation: 'Smuasach' – the nose. Dinneen.

Also 'Bainim smuasach as – I knock sparks out of him, beat
violently'. Dinneen.

SMUSH, noun

Small pieces, smithereens.

Use: The vase fell and was broken into smush =
The vase fell and broke into small pieces.

Derivation: 'Smush' – anything reduced to small fine fragments. Joyce.

SOCK, verb

To strike, to beat, especially in the case of a school-teacher punishing a pupil by striking on the hands with a stick.

Use: The teacher socked me =
The teacher struck me with a stick on the hands (palms).

Derivation: 'Sock' – to strike. Concise Oxford Dictionary.

SOOLUCK, noun

Dirty soapy water, also effluent.

Use: The water was in sooluck after him =
The water was very dirty after he washed himself.

Derivation: 'Súlach' – juice, sap, suds. 'Súlach na buaile – liquid farmyard manure'. Dinneen.

SOOT, noun

Satisfaction, pleasure (used in negative context)

Use: I wouldn't give him the soot of it =
I wouldn't give him the satisfaction of having it.

Derivation: Doubtful, but perhaps 'Sotal'. 'Ní raibh mé faoi shotal ar bith dó – I did not give way to him in the least'. Dinneen.

SOUR, ON, verb
To inform (on a person), to betray.
Use: He soured on me =
He informed on me.
Derivation: Unknown, but probably related to sour or acid taste, hence to feel bitter, to inform.

SPADGY, noun
A sparrow.
Derivation: Possibly 'Spideóg' – a robin, a small bird. Dinneen.
Note English 'Spadgy' (slang) – sparrow. Oxford English Dictionary.
German 'Spatz' – a sparrow. Cassells.

SPOGGER, noun
A peaked cap.
Use: He had his spogger in his pocket =
He had his (peaked) cap in his pocket.
Derivation unknown.

SPONDULICKS, noun
Money.
Derivation: Unknown, 19th century slang. Concise Oxford Dictionary.

SPRAZZY, noun
Sixpence (old money).
Derivation: Note Shelta 'Sprazi' – a sixpence. MacAlister.
Possibly from 'Sprat' – a sixpence (pre-1839). Partridge.

SPUR, noun
Insane / blind
Use: He's going spur =
He's losing his sanity.
Derivation: Possibly Old English 'Spur' – to get drunk, hence
lose control. Partridge.

STALL, noun and verb
Love-making.
Use: I had a great stall last night =
I had a grand 'court' last night.
Derivation: Possibly Irish 'Stail' – a stallion, but figuratively –
a gay spark, a paramour. Dinneen.

STAND, noun
A reward, a tip.
Use: He did me out of a stand as nice as you like =
He cheated me out of a tip as adroitly as you could
imagine. Murphy.
Derivation unknown.

STAVE, noun
A song.
Use: Give us a stave ! =
Give us a song.
Derivation: Probably from 'Staff' (musical).

"A Stare"

STEAMER, noun

A cigarette.

Use: Have you a steamer?
Have you a cigarette?

Derivation: 'Stimire' – a pipe, tobacco pipe. 'Béarlagar na saer'. MacAlister.

Also Shelta 'Stima' – steamer, tobacco pipe. MacAlister.

STEAMER, noun

Homosexual person (male).

Use: He's a steamer =
He is a homosexual.

Derivation unknown.

STEERINAH, noun

A 'steering' car, a boy's home-made toy cart. There were two versions, the most usual being constructed from a timber plank about 18" wide and 24" to 36" long. The wheels were attached to the ends of two battens which were fitted to the underside of the plank at front and rear. The front batten was loosely fitted so that it swivelled and the cart was steered by pulling on strings attached to the ends of the batten projecting beyond the sides of the plank.

STOCKING, noun

A lot of money.

Use: She has a good stocking =
She has a lot of money.

Derivation: Note Old English 'A store of money'. Partridge.

N.B. Dealers on Coal Quay invariably kept paper money inside their stockings, hence 'stocking'.

STRAP, noun
Credit, tick (see 'Slate').
Use: Our local publican is good for strap =
Our local publican will give credit.
Derivation: Unknown, possibly Old English. Partridge.

STRAP, noun
Strong, big person (usually applied to a girl).
Use: She's a fine strap of a girl =
She's a fine big girl.
Derivation: Irish 'Strapaire' (cailín) – a vigorous well-built girl. Dinneen.
Also English 'Strap' – big, lusty, tall. Concise Oxford Dictionary.

STRAWK-HAWL, verb
To fish illegally with line and three hooks. See 'Puck'.
Derivation: Unknown, but probably a corruption of 'Stroke-haul'.
and note "The 'stroke-all' of fishing was known as a 'straw-call' to older Corkonians". Ó h-Ealuithe.
and 'Strokehaul'. Murphy.

STRAWK HAWLING, An expression of satisfaction with oneself and life in reply to an enquiry about one's health, etc., an expression of good-humoured resignation.
Use: How're you doing?
Answer: Strawkhawlin'!
Derivation: Unknown, but note 'Struggling to make a living, just managing'. 'Strácáil' – dragging, drudging. Ó h-Ealuithe.

94

STROKE, noun
A good appetite.
Use: He has a huge stroke =
He has an enormous appetite.
Derivation unknown.

STROKE, TO PULL A, noun
To play a trick, to outwit (see 'Fast-one').
Use: He pulled a stroke on the bookies =
He tricked the bookmakers.
Derivation: Unknown, but note 'a feat, an achievement'.
Chambers.
Possibly cognate with 'Stroke' – the oarsman who sits on the
bench next to the coxswain and sets the stroke of the oars.
Brewer.

STUMER, noun
A foolish person.
Use: He's a stumer =
He's a foolish person.
Derivation: Doubtful, but note Shelta 'Stimra' – a ragged
begging vagrant. MacAlister.
'Stumer' – counterfeit coin or note, fraud, failure (19th
century) origin unknown. Concise Oxford Dictionary.

TABS, TO KEEP . . . . ON
To keep an eye on, to keep under surveillance.
Use: You'd want to keep tabs on that fellow =
You'd want to keep a sharp eye on him.
Derivation unknown.

TACK, noun
Sixpence.
Use: Two and a tack.
Two shillings and sixpence.
Derivation unknown.

TACK
None (emphasis).
Use: "There's no fear I'll ever pay a tack of attention to ye". =
There is no fear that I'll pay any notice to you. Murphy.
Derivation unknown.

TACK, TO GO ON THE
To become teetotal.
Use: I'm going on the tack for Lent =
I'm giving up the drink during Lent.
Derivation: English military (late 1920). Partridge.

TANNER, noun
A sixpenny piece (old coin).
Use: He gave me a tanner =
He gave me sixpence.
Derivation: English slang 'a Tanner' (no origin). Concise
Oxford Dictionary.
and Gipsy 'Tawno' – little one.
Italian 'Danaro' – small changer. Brewer.
Old English. Partridge.

TAP, verb
To beg, to touch (which see).
Use: He tapped me for a sprazi =
He begged a sixpence from me.
Derivation: 'Tap' – to apply to, to solicit. Concise Oxford
Dictionary.
On the tap, begging for money. Partridge

TAPE, verb

To take one's measure, to size up (figurative sense).
Use: I have him taped all right =
I have taken his measure.
Derivation: Possibly military – taping the lines of advance in the First World War.
or Old English 'Taeppe' (slang) – to sum up. Concise Oxford Dictionary.

TARRY-BOY, noun

A male of questionable behaviour (amorous person).
Use: He's a tarry-boy! =
He's a randy individual
Derivation: Unknown, but note Irish 'Tarbh' and Latin 'Taurus' – a bull.

TASPEY or TASPY, noun

Ardour, high spirits.
Use: He has great taspy on him =
He is in high spirits.
Derivation: Probably Irish 'Teaspach' – literally ardour, fury. Ó Domhnaill.
'Tesbach' – ardour, fury. Greene & Quin.

TAW, noun

A large clay marble, usually brightly coloured, used in game of marbles (which see).
Derivation: Unknown, but possibly 18th century English. Concise Oxford Dictionary.

TAW, UP ON YOUR

An exclamation – face up to the challenge.

Use: Up on your taws now =
You must now face the challenge.

Derivation: See 'Taw' above.

TAWRNEEN, noun

Small fish – minnow, pinkeen, a thorn-back. Tawrneens are caught either in net or by worm tied to end of string.

Derivation: Unknown, but note thorn on spine of fish and 'een' diminutive in Irish.

and note 'Tairnín' or 'Tairngín' – a small nail, a thorn-back. Ó h-Ealuithe.

THUNDER UP THE GULLEY

A game practised by boys. Paper was stuffed up a cast-iron downpipe and set on fire producing a loud roaring sound. Derivation unknown.

TICK, noun and verb

Credit, slate, (which see).

Use: There isn't a shop in Cork that would give that fellow tick =
He cannot get credit in any shop in Cork.

Derivation: A colloquialism, an abbreviation of 'on the ticket' – credit. Concise Oxford Dictionary.

TILLY, noun

A small quantity (of liquid) provided by the supplier in addition to the standard measure (term usually employed with reference to milk supply in the days when milk was distributed out of churns).

Derivation: Probably Irish 'Tuilleadh' – act of addition to or increasing. Dinneen.

'Tilly' – something additional and of small value given into the bargain as a gift or bonus.

A small ewer of milk given to a servant by a milkman over and above that for use by the family. Wright.

TISOVERITEYE or TISOVEREYETYE

It is in front of you, it is directly in front of you.

Derivation: Corruption and confusion of various words. 'Ós do chomhair amach' – in front of you and 'Cóir' – right. Joyce.

and note 'Saucepan came into the kitchen in his stocking vamps and disgraced us overright the strange woman'. Murphy.

TOD(D), OUT ON HIS

Incomparable, supreme, splendid.

Use: He was out on his tod(d) as a player =
He was excellent as a player.

Derivation: 'Todd' – one's own, alone. Perhaps rhyming slang – on one's Tod Sloan. Concise Oxford Dictionary.

Alone – to work alone. Partridge.

TODDY, HOT

A drink, a mixture of whiskey, boiling water, honey or sugar and cloves.

Derivation: Doubtful, but note 'The word is a corruption of 'Taudi' the Indian name for the saccharine juice of palm spathes'. Brewer.

TONGUE, noun
'Music' (which see) of harrier dogs.
Derivation: 'Tongue' – sound.

TOSSER, noun
Implement (usually piece of slate, matchbox, cigarette box or hair comb) used while tossing coins in 'Feck' and 'Bee-up' (which see).
Derivation: Verb to toss.

TOSSER, noun
Money, means (used in a negative sense).
Use: I havn't a tosser =
I have no money.
Derivation unknown.

TOUCH, noun and verb
To cadge, beg.
Use: He touched me for a £1 =
He asked me for a £1.
Derivation: English, somewhat obscure, but see 'Touch' – to get sum out of. Concise Oxford Dictionary.

TOY, noun
Ironic expression – undesirable person.
Use: She's a nice toy =
She is not a nice person.
Derivation unknown.

TRAPS, noun

Belongings, baggage.

Use: He left the house with his traps =
He left the house with his belongings.

Derivation: Related to 'Trappings', also French 'Drap' – clothes. Concise Oxford Dictionary.

TRÁWNEEN, noun

Of little value or importance.

Use: It (he / she) isn't worth a tráwneen =
It isn't worth anything.

Derivation: Irish 'Tráithnín' – strong blade of grass. Dinneen.

TRIBLER, noun

To win three tricks in game of 'Niner' (which see).

Use: Stop the tribler or we'll have to pay doublers =
Stop him winning the three tricks or we'll have to pay him
double the stakes.

Derivation: 'Trebul' – triple, threefold. Greene, Quin.

TRIPE, noun

Lining of sheep's stomach (Cork delicacy cooked in milk with onions, butter and pepper).

Derivation unknown.

TRIPES, TO CUT THE . . . . . . OUT OF

To criticise severely.

Use: I cut the tripes out of him =
I criticised him severely.

Derivation: Unknown, but see 'Tripe' above, possibly extended meaning of entrails.

TROT, ON THE
In succession.

Use: We won the County three times on the trot =
We won the County Championship on three successive
occasions.

Derivation: Unknown, but note 'A succession of heads thrown at two-up'. Partridge.

TROTTER, noun
A term used in the card games (Three- and Nine-card Brag) to describe three cards in numerical sequence).

Derivation: Unknown, but see 'Trot, on the'.

TRUMMER, noun
A threepenny coin (3d. now obsolete).

Derivation unknown.

TRUCK, noun
Participation, association (used in a negative sense).

Use: Don't have any truck with that fellow =
Don't have any contact (business) with that fellow.

Derivation: 'Trucail' – a cart, a sidecar. Dinneen.

Note 'With whom we trafficked and trucked'. Alex the Coppersmith.

'Avoid dealing with'. Concise Oxford Dictionary.

'Truck' – exchange, business trade. Wright.

TULLOCK, noun
A blow.

Use: I gave him a tullock =
I gave him a dig (which see).

Derivation: Irish 'Tolg' – an attack. Greene, Quin.

TWANG, noun

Accent (usually applied as a derogatory term to English and American accents affected by some Cork people on returning home after a comparatively short stay abroad).

Derivation unknown.

TWIG, TO, verb

To understand.

Use: You twig?
You understand?

Derivation: Possibly Irish 'Tuig' – to understand.

and note 'Twig' – a divining rod for water, hence by extension 'understanding'. Wright.

and also 'Twig' – I catch your meaning, I understand (Irish 'Tuigim' – I notice). Brewer.

UCKS, noun

Apple core.

Use: I'm up the ucks =
I'll take (and eat) the core of the apple.

Derivation unknown.

VAMPS, STOCKIN'

The soles of the feet (in stockings).

Use: He was six feet two (inches) in his stockin' vamps =
He stood six feet two inches standing in his stockings i.e.
without shoes.

Derivation: See 'Vamp' (corruption of meaning).

and note 'Saucepan came into the kitchen in his stockin' vamps and disgraced us overright the strange woman'. Murphy.

VAMP, verb

To walk.

Use: He vamped from Cork to Crosser =
He walked from Cork to Crosshaven.

Derivation: 'Vamp' – upper front part of boot or shoe, hence to walk.

Middle English from Anglo French 'Vampé', Old French 'Avant pié' ('Avant – before, see 'Avaunt' – pied foot). Concise Oxford Dictionary.

WAGON, FEED THE

Play for safety. A sporting term (usually means to kick the ball out of the field of play).

Derivation unknown.

WAGONS MORE

Lots more.

Use: Help yourself to a sandwich, there's wagons more =
Help yourself to a sandwich, there's plenty more.

Derivation: Unknown, but possible association of wagon with a large quantity of goods.

WAMMON, noun

A huge fish.

Use: I caught a wammon up the Lough yesterday =
I caught a huge fish in the Lough yesterday.

Derivation unknown.

WAN, noun

A female (derogatory).

Use: That wan, is it? =
That one is no good.

Derivation: Probably a corruption of 'One' or 'Wan' – thin. Anglo-Saxon 'Wan' – deficient. Brewer.

WAN, OLD
The mother (affectionate).
Use: His old wan died =
His mother died.
Derivation: Doubtful, but see above.

WASH, noun
Organic refuse used as food for pigs. The 'wash' of each house was collected (sometimes paid for) and fed to the collector's own pigs or sold on to farmers.
Derivation: English. Chambers.

WASH, noun
Sustain (argument, case) used in a negative context.
Use: That won't wash =
That cannot be sustained.
Derivation: Probably 18th or 19th Century English. Chambers.

Waxing
a Gaza

WAUGH-MOUTH, HAVE A, noun

To speak too much. A person who cannot keep a secret.

Use: He has a waugh-mouth =
   He cannot keep a secret.

Derivation: Unknown, but possibly association between open mouth and inability to refrain from speech.

WAX, verb

To climb, shin up a pipe or pole.

Use: To wax a gaza (which see) =
   To climb up a gas lamp.

Derivation: Unknown, but possibly from 'Wax' – to grow.

and note 'Wax-flower' – a climbing plant. Chambers.

WEIGHT, noun

A measure of weight equal to 7 lbs. (usually of potatoes).
3½ lbs.=a half-weight.

Use: I'll take a weight of potatoes =
I'll take 7 lbs. of potatoes.

Derivation unknown.

WELLINGTONS (BOOTS), noun

Russian boots (which see).

WHACK, IN, noun

In partnership, equal share (generally related to business).

Use: We were in w(h)ack =
We were in partnership.
also
He did more than his w(h)ack of work =
He did more than his share of work.

Derivation: Unknown, but note 'Whack (share) of pleasure'.
Concise Oxford Dictionary.

WHACKED, verb

Tired, exhausted.

Use: I'm whacked =
I'm exhausted.

Derivation unknown.

WHACKER, noun

A measure of volume related to alcohol (almost always brandy). Half a half-glass.

Use: A whacker of brandy, please.

Derivation: Unknown, but possibly related to 'In whack' (which see).

BIBLIOGRAPHY

Alexander the Coppersmith	*Remarks upon the Religion, Trade, Government, Police, Customs and Maladys of the City of Corke*
T. O. Bartley	*Teague, Shenkin and Sawney*
A. Bliss	*Spoken English in Ireland, 1600 – 1740*
E. Brady	*All in, All in!*
M. Ó Briain	*Cnósach Focal ó Bhaile Bhúirne*
B. Ó Cuiv	*The Irish of West Muskerry, County Cork*
D. Ó h-Éaluithe	*Irish Words in Cork Speech. Cork Historical & Archaeological Journal, Vol. 49., 1944*
P. W. Joyce	*English as it is Spoken in Ireland*
D. L. Kelleher	*Cork's Own Town*
T. Lehane	*Cork's Own Town*
R.A.S. MacAlister	*Secret Languages of Ireland*
B. MacMahon	*The Honeyspike*
T. P. O'Mahony	*The Klondyke Memorial*
S. Murphy	*Stone Mad*
N. Tóibín	*A Poem (see appendix)*

DICTIONARIES

T. De Bhaldraithe	*English-Irish Dictionary*
E. C. Brewer	*The Dictionary of Phrase and Fable*
Cassells	*Compact French-English Dictionary*
Cassells	*German-English Dictionary*
Chambers	*20th Century Dictionary*
P. S. Dinneen	*Foclóir Gaeilge 7 Béarla*
N. Ó Domhnaill	*Foclóir Gaelge 7 Béarla*
K. Meyer	*Contribution to Irish Lexicography*
	Compact Oxford Dictionary
	Concise Oxford Dictionary
	Shorter Oxford English Dictionary
E. Partridge	*Dictionary of Slang and Unconventional English*
J. Wright	*English Dialect Dictionary*

ROYAL IRISH ACADEMY DICTIONARY OF OLD AND MIDDLE IRISH

A. *Contributions to a Dictionary of the Irish Language*
Anna O'Sullivan, E. G. Quin

B. *Contributions to a Dictionary of the Irish Language*
Maire Carney, Máirín Ó Daly

C. (3 parts) *Contributions to a Dictionary of the Irish Language*
Proinnsias Ní Cheathain, Máirín Ó Daly, P. Ó Fiannachta,
Anna O'Sullivan

D. – Degoir *Dictionary of the Irish Language*
Carl. J. Marstrander
Degoir – *Dictionary of the Irish Language*
Mary E. Byrne, Maud Joynt

E. *Dictionary of the Irish Language*
Maud Joynt, Eleanor Knott

F. – Focraic *Dictionary of the Irish Language*
Maud Joynt, Eleanor Knott
Foc-Futha – *Dictionary of the Irish Language*
Maud Joynt, Eleanor Knott

G. *Contributions to a Dictionary of the Irish Language*
Mary E. Byrne

H. *Contributions to a Dictionary of the Irish Language*
Mary Carney

I. – Imnah *Contributions to a Dictionary of the Irish Language*
Máirín Ó Daly, Anna O'Sullivan
Imnam – *Contributions to a Dictionary of the Irish Language*
Máirín Ó Daly, Anna O'Sullivan

L. *Contributions to a Dictionary of the Irish Language*
Máirín Ó Daly, P. Ó Fiannachta

M. *Contributions to a Dictionary of the Irish Language*
Maud Joynt

N.O.P. *Contributions to a Dictionary of the Irish Language*
Maud Joynt

R. *Contributions to a Dictionary of the Irish Language*
Maud Joynt

S. *Contributions to a Dictionary of the Irish Language*
Maud Joynt, Teresa Condon, Máirín Ó Daly, Anna O'Sullivan
(E. G. Quin, General Editor)

T. – Tnuthaigid *Contributions to a Dictionary of the Irish Language*
David Greene, E. G. Quin
To – Tu *Contributions to a Dictionary of the Irish Language*
David Greene, E. G. Quin

U. *Contributions to a Dictionary of the Irish Language*
Teresa Condon

CORK

Cork is also Johnny Quirke
  Timothy Jim and Florrie Burke,
Cork is Lavitt's Quay's Mná
  Daly's Bridge and Andy Gaw.
Cork is Statia, Hannah Pidge
  Mullet under Patrick's Bridge,
Knuckles steaming on a dish
  Cafflers who strawkhaul for fish.
Railway engines on the street
  Close to where two rivers meet,
Cork is murky, foggy, funny
  Scintillating, sad and sunny.
Where young Seánie, Gunk and Chaazer
  Ask the barber for a bazer,
Not a thing however strange'll
  E'er perturb the Goldy Angel.
Cork is lofty, sprawling Gurran,
  Toffee-apples and brown dawn,
Cork is goitre, gawk and ire,
  The Butterah, the Four-faced Liar.
Cork is silence one an' all
  Order for a noble call,
Tongues and tails and fivers wag
  In Killeens when there's a drag.
And good old Drummer and Ceolán
  Sniff the trail they laid at dawn,
Crosser, Mikes and Piper's Merries,
  Planks of luscious ripe blackberries.
Cork is tadpoles and thorneens
  Battle-board and sweet drisheens,
Cork, as like as not, is what'll
  Quickly be whipped off the bottle.
'Till Paddy be dished out in dollops
  For the men from the Metrollops,
Cork is maybe, I agree
  Not cracked what it's cracked up to be.
But, brother, even if it's not
  It's still the best of what we've got.

Courtesy of Niall Tóibín

111

Aish, e:ʃ

Baa, all a, a:l ə ba:

Back, own, o:n bak

Back-beril, bak berl̩

Bake, bek

Band-house player, *

Bareaas, 'be:raz

Banks, down the, dəun də baŋks

Basket, baskət

Bate, ba:t

Battle-board, batl̩ - bo:rd

Batter, batər

Baytur, be:tər

Bazer, be:zər

Bazz, baz

Bazzer, bazər

Bellisit upum, beləsətopəm

Bee-up, bi:əp

Beril, berl̩

Bing-bing, biŋ - biŋ

Blackas, blak a:z

Bockety, bakəti:

Bodice, badəs

Bolger, baldʒər

Book, buk

Bowls, game of, ge.m əv boulz

Bowl, long, laŋ boul

Bowl of odds, boul əv adz

Box, on the, an də baks

Brag, three-card, tri: kard brag

Brassed-off, brast af

Brasser, brasər

Browl, broul

Brus, bros

Brus, „

Burn, born

Butt, bot

Caffler, kaflər

Call, ka:l

Call, „

Call, a noble, ə no: bl̩ ka:l

Call, ka:l

Call, „

Cat and dog, kat ən dag

Carrrying, kari-iŋ

Cawhake, ka:he:k

Cawhake, „

Chaneys, 'tʃe:ni:z

Chaney-eye, 'tʃe:ni:ai

Chaw, to .... out, tə tʃa: əut

Choicer, tʃaisər

Claim, kle:m

Click, klik

Cling, kliŋ

Clod, klad

Clout, kləut

Cobbage, kabidʒ

Cocker, kakər

Cod, kad

Codger, kadʒər

Collar, kalər

Collops, kaləps

Conjun-box, kanʒən - baks

Connihaly, kani:he:li:

Connishur, kanəʃu:r

Cop on (to), kap an

Cottage, kátədʒ

Cough, to soften, tə safən k(

Cowluck, kəulək

Crabbit, krabət

Crackawly, kráka:li:

Craw-sick, kra:sik

Dafake, da:fe:k

Dalk, da:k

Danti-dan, danti - dan

Daw, da:

Dawn, brown, brun da:n

Daza, me, mi da:za

Dead man, ded man

Dead man, „

* band haus ple:r

112

Dekko (or dekho), **deko**
Didlum, **didləm**
Dig, **dig**
Dig,   **"**
Dinger, **diŋər**
Dog, black **blak dag**
Dollop, **daləp**
Don, **dan**
Don, small, **smɑ:l dan**
Don, big, **big dan**
Donkey's gudge, **daŋki:z gudʒ**
Donkey's   **daŋki:z**
Wedding cake, **wedin ke:k**
Dooshie, **du:ʃi**
Dowtchaboy, **dəu'tʃə bai**
Drag or
Draghunt, **drag, drag hont**
Drag, to run **tə ron**
a . . . . with, **ə drag wit**
Drag, to run
a . . . . with,
Drisheen, **driʃi:n**
Drop, **drap**
Drop, bad, **bad drap**
Dropsy, **'drapsi:**
Duck, **dok**
Dust, **dost**
Dust,   **"**
Fakin, **fe:kən**
Fast-one, **fast wan**
Feck, **fek**
Fecking around, **fekin əraund**
Flah, **fla:**
Flah-bag, **fla: bag**
Flahed out, **fla:d əut**
Flake, **fle:k**
Fly, **flai**
Fly,   **"**
Fooder, **fu:dər**
Fooster, **fu:stər**

Foxer, **faksər**
Funt, **funt**
Gallon, **galən**
Gallon (to get
one's),   **"**
Gander, **gandər**
Gash, **gaʃ**
Gatch, **gɑ:tʃ**
Gattle, **gatəl**
Gauzer, **gɑ:zər**
Gawk, **gɑ:k**
Gawk,   **"**
Gaza, **gɑ:za**
Geanc, **gjunk**
Gee-up, **dʒi:'op**
Giddum, **gidəm**
Glassey alley, **glasi:'ali:**
Glawm, **glɑ:m**
Gligeen, **gligi:n**
Gobble-job, **gabəl dʒab**
Gobs, game of, **gabz**
Gobs,   **"**
mouthful of, **moutfəl av gabz**
Gom, **gam**
Gonon strips, **go:nən strips**
Goosah, to play, **gu:za**
Gowl, **gəul**
Gowl,   **"**
Grass, **gras**
Grig, **grig**
Guiner, **gainər**
Gully, **guli**
Gurrey, **guri**
Gutty (boy), **guti**
Guzz-eye, **guz ai**
Guzzle, **guzəl**
Gwall, **gwɑ:l**
H.L.I., **he:tʃ el ai**
Hack, **hak**
Hastener, **he:snər**

113

Half, fine, **fain haːf**
Hanging, **haŋin**
Heap, to be up
in a . . . ., **tə bi əp in a hiːp**
Higos, a touch **haiguz,**
of the . . . . ., **a tutʃ əv də.......**
Higo shytes, **haigo ʃaits**
Hise, **hais**
Hobble, **habəl**
Hoofler, **huːflər**
Hop, on the, **hap**
Hop off, **hap af**
Hop, a . . . off **tə hav ə hap af**
to have,
Ire, **oir**
Ire, **"**
Ire, a touch of, **totʃ av oir**
Jack, **dʒak**
Jag, **dʒag**
Jibber, **dʒibər**
Jockey, **dʒakiː**
Jolly, **dʒaliː**
Jorum, **dʒoːrəm**
Joulter, **dʒəultər**
Jub-jubs, **dʒub-dʒubz**
Karroge, **kaːroːg**
Kick, **kik**
Kick, **"**
Kilter, out of **kiltər**
Kisser, **kisər**
Knacker, **nakər**
Knawvshawling, **'naːvʃaːlin**
Kybosh, **kai baʃ**
Lace, **leːs**
Lang, on the **laŋ**
Langer, **laŋər**
Langer, **"**
Langers, **laŋərz**
Lag, **lag**
Lamp, **lamp**

Land, **land**
Lash, **laʃ**
Lash, **"**
Lash-up, **'laʃ op**
Lasher, **laʃər**
Ledder, **ledər**
Levit, **levət**
Lick up to, **tə lik əp tə**
Lick, or lick
into a fit, **tc tə lik intə ə fit**
Line, doing a, **duːiŋ a lain**
Lip, to have
a . . . for, **lip**
Lip, to have **"**
a . . . on,
Lop, **lop**
Losset, **losət**
Lowry, **'lauriː**
Mala, **maːlə**
Manky, **'maŋkiː**
Manage, **manədʒ**
Mark, **mark**
Masher, **maʃər**
Massive, **masəv**
Mauser, **maːzər**
Mawkish, **maːkəʃ**
Meb, **meb**
Mebs, **mebs**
Mebs, **"**
Meejum, **miːdʒəm**
Mockeyah, **makiːjaː**
Mockeen **makiːn**
Moolah, **'muːlaː**
Moreran, **'moːrər an**
Moylow, **'moilo**
Mug, **mog**
Mullacker, **'moləqər**
Music, **'mjuːzək**
Napper, **napər**
National, **'naʃənəl**

114

Niner,	nainər	Sconce,	skans
Noodeenaw,	'nu:dəna:	Scoot-eye,	sku:t - ai
Nooks,	nu:ks	Score,	sko:ɹ
Odds, milk and,	adz	Scove,	sko:v
One,	wun	Scrip,	skrip
Out, to be had,	out	Scuttling,	skotlin
Ownshuck,	'o:nʃək	Septic,	septək
Paralatic,	'pɑrɑlatək	Sham,	ʃam
Pain, out of,	pe:n	Shaper,	ʃe:pər
Pana, doing,	pa:nə	Sheefra,	ʃi:frə
Pavi,	'pa:vi:	Shellityhorn	ʃelitə'ha:rn
Pawny,	'pa:ni:	Sherang,	ʃe'raŋ
Pickey,	'piki:	Shlowny,	'ʃlouni:
Pitch,	pitʃ	Showery,	'ʃouri:
Pizawn,	paiza:n	Skalp,	skalp
Plain,	ple:n	Skelp,	skelp
Plank,	plank	Skeog,	skjag
Plank,	„	Skeory,	'skio:ri:
Pole, up the,	po:l	Skite,	skoit
Ponney,	'pani:	Skites,	skaits
Pontoon,	pantu:n	Skull,	skol
Pooley,	'pu:li	Slag,	slag
Poxed,	pakst	Slate,	sle:t
Priell,	prail	Slates, away for,	sle:ts
Puck,	pok	Slob,	slab
Puck,	„	Slock	slak
Puss,	pus	(Slocking),	slakin
Queer-hawk,	kwe:r ha:k	Slog,	slag
Rack,	rak	Slug,	slog
Rake, a,	re:k	Smack,	smak
Ranker,	raŋər	Smathers, to	rankər
Razz,	raz	make . . . . of	smjadərz
Reck,	rek	Smush,	ʒmuʃ
Rider,	raidər	Smush,	„
Rotto,	ratə	Sock,	sak
Rubber dollies	robər - dali:z	Sooluck,	su:lək
Ructions,	rokʃənz	Soot,	sut
Sawney,	'sa:ni:	Sour, on,	saur
Scauld,	sca:ld	Spadgy,	'spadʒi
Scatter, to cut a	skatər	Spogger,	spagər

115

Spondulicks,	spandu:ləks	Toss,	tas
Sprazzy,	'sprazi:	Tosser,	tasər
Spur,	spor	Tosser,	"
Stall,	sta:l	Touch,	totʃ
Steerinah,	sti:rə'na	Toy,	toi
Stand,	stand	Traps,	traps
Stave,	ste:v	Trawneen,	tra:ni:n
Steamer,	sti:mər	Tribler,	'triblər
Steamer,	"	Tripe,	traip
Stocking,	stakən	Tripes, to cut	
Strap,	strap	the . . . . out of,	traips
Strap,	"	Trot, on the	trat
Strawk hawling,	stra:k-ha:lən	Trotter,	tratər
Strawk-hawl,	stra:k-hal	Trummer,	tromər
Stroke,	stro:k	Truck,	trok
Stroke, to	"	Tullock,	toløk
pull a,		Twang,	twaŋ
Stumer,	stju:mər	Twig, to,	twig
Tabs, to	tabz	Ucks,	oks
keep . . . . on,		Vamps, stockin',	'stakin vams
Tack,	tak	Vamp,	vamp
Tack,	"	Wagon, feed the,	fi:d de wagən
Tack, go on the,	"	Wagons more,	wagənz mo:r
Tanner,	tanər	Wammon,	wamən
Tap,	tap	Wan,	wan
Tape,	te:p	Wan, old,	oul wan
Tarry-boy,	'ta:ri-bai	Wash,	waʃ
Taspey or		Wash,	"
Taspy,	'taspi:	Waugh-mouth,	wa: maut̯
Taw,	ta:	have a,	
Taw, up on your	ta:	Wax,	waks
Tawr-neen,	'ta:rni:n	Weight,	we:t
Thunder up		Wellingtons,	weliŋtənz
the gulley,	'tundər op de goli:	Whack, in,	wak
Tick,	tik	Whacked,	whakt
Tilly,	'tili:	Whacker,	'wakər
Tisoveriteye,	tizo:vəraitju		
Tod(d), out of his,	tad		
Toddy, hot,	'tadi:		
Tongue,	tuŋ		